CENSORSHIP

Opposing Viewpoints

Other Books of Related Interest in the Opposing Viewpoints Series:

Sexual Values
Social Justice
American Values

Additional Books in the Opposing Viewpoints Series:

American Foreign Policy
The American Military
America's Prisons
The Arms Race
Censorship
Central America
Chemical Dependency
Constructing a Life Philosophy
Crime & Criminals
Criminal Justice
Death & Dying
The Ecology Controversy
The Energy Crisis
Male/Female Roles
The Middle East
The Political Spectrum
Problems of Death
Religion and Human Experience
Science and Religion
The Welfare State
The Vietnam War
War and Human Nature

CENSORSHIP

Opposing Viewpoints

David L. Bender & Bruno Leone, Series Editors

Terry O'Neill, Book Editor

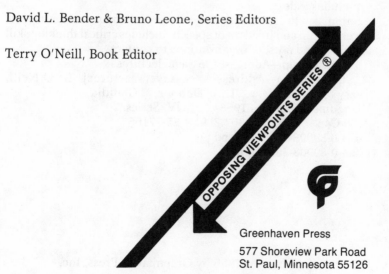

OPPOSING VIEWPOINTS SERIES ®

Greenhaven Press
577 Shoreview Park Road
St. Paul, Minnesota 55126

Library of Congress Cataloging-in-Publication Data
Main entry under title:

Censorship, opposing viewpoints.

(Opposing viewpoints series)
Bibliography: p.
Includes index.
Summary: Presents opposing viewpoints about various aspects of censorship and freedom of speech. Includes critical thinking skill activities and a list of organizations to contact.

1. Censorship—Addresses, essays, lectures.
[1. Censorship—Addresses, essays, lectures] I. O'Neill, Terry, 1944-   . II. Debner, Claudia, 1951-
III. Szumski, Bonnie, 1958-   . IV. Series.
Z659.C46   1985   302.2′4   85-17165
ISBN 0-89908-377-3 (lib. bdg.)
ISBN 0-89908-352-8 (pbk.)

"Congress shall make no law . . . abridging the freedom of speech, or of the press."

First Amendment to the US Constitution

The basic foundation of our democracy is the first amendment guarantee of freedom of expression. The *Opposing Viewpoints Series* is dedicated to the concept of this basic freedom and the idea that it is more important to practice it than to enshrine it.

Contents

Chapter 3: Does National Security Justify Censorship?

Chapter 4: Is School and Library Censorship Justified?

Chapter 5: Should Pornography Be Censored?

Why Consider Opposing Viewpoints?

"It is better to debate a question without settling it than to settle a question without debating it."

Joseph Joubert (1754-1824)

The Importance of Examining Opposing Viewpoints

The purpose of the Opposing Viewpoints Series, and this book in particular, is to present balanced, and often difficult to find, opposing points of view on complex and sensitive issues.

Probably the best way to become informed is to analyze the positions of those who are regarded as experts and well studied on issues. It is important to consider every variety of opinion in an attempt to determine the truth. Opinions from the mainstream of society should be examined. But also important are opinions that are considered radical, reactionary, or minority as well as those stigmatized by some other uncomplimentary label. An important lesson of history is the eventual acceptance of many unpopular and even despised opinions. The ideas of Socrates, Jesus, and Galileo are good examples of this.

Readers will approach this book with their own opinions on the issues debated within it. However, to have a good grasp of one's own viewpoint, it is necessary to understand the arguments of those with whom one disagrees. It can be said that those who do not completely understand their adversary's point of view do not fully understand their own.

9

A persuasive case for considering opposing viewpoints has been presented by John Stuart Mill in his work *On Liberty*. When examining controversial issues it may be helpful to reflect on this suggestion:

> The only way in which a human being can make some approach to knowing the whole of a subject, is by hearing what can be said about it by persons of every variety of opinion, and studying all modes in which it can be looked at by every character of mind. No wise man ever acquired his wisdom in any mode but this.

Analyzing Sources of Information

The Opposing Viewpoints Series includes diverse materials taken from magazines, journals, books, and newspapers, as well as statements and position papers from a wide range of individuals, organizations and governments. This broad spectrum of sources helps to develop patterns of thinking which are open to the consideration of a variety of opinions.

Pitfalls to Avoid

A pitfall to avoid in considering opposing points of view is that of regarding one's own opinion as being common sense and the most rational stance and the point of view of others as being only opinion and naturally wrong. It may be that another's opinion is correct and one's own is in error.

Another pitfall to avoid is that of closing one's mind to the opinions of those with whom one disagrees. The best way to approach a dialogue is to make one's primary purpose that of understanding the mind and arguments of the other person and not that of enlightening him or her with one's own solutions. More can be learned by listening than speaking.

It is my hope that after reading this book the reader will have a deeper understanding of the issues debated and will appreciate the complexity of even seemingly simple issues on which good and honest people disagree. This awareness is particularly important in a democratic society such as ours where people enter into public debate to determine the common good. Those with whom one disagrees should not necessarily be regarded as enemies, but perhaps simply as people who suggest different paths to a common goal.

Developing Basic Reading and Thinking Skills

In this book, carefully edited opposing viewpoints are purposely placed back to back to create a running debate; each viewpoint is preceded by a short quotation that best expresses the author's main argument. This format instantly plunges the reader into the midst of a controversial issue and greatly aids that reader in mastering the basic skill of recognizing an author's point of view.

A number of basic skills for critical thinking are practiced in the activities that appear throughout the books in the series. Some of the skills are:

Evaluating Sources of Information The ability to choose from among alternative sources the most reliable and accurate source in relation to a given subject.

Separating Fact from Opinion The ability to make the basic distinction between factual statements (those that can be demonstrated or verified empirically) and statements of opinion (those that are beliefs or attitudes that cannot be proved).

Identifying Stereotypes The ability to identify oversimplified, exaggerated descriptions (favorable or unfavorable) about people and insulting statements about racial, religious or national groups, based upon misinformation or lack of information.

Recognizing Ethnocentrism The ability to recognize attitudes or opinions that express the view that one's own race, culture, or group is inherently superior, or those attitudes that judge another culture or group in terms of one's own.

It is important to consider opposing viewpoints and equally important to be able to critically analyze those viewpoints. The activities in this book are designed to help the reader master these thinking skills. Statements are taken from the book's viewpoints and the reader is asked to analyze them. This technique aids the reader in developing skills that not only can be applied to the viewpoints in this book, but also to situations where opinionated spokespersons comment on controversial issues. Although the activities are helpful to the solitary reader, they are most useful when the reader can benefit from the interaction of group discussion.

Using this book and others in the series should help readers develop basic reading and thinking skills. These skills should improve the reader's ability to understand what they read. Readers should be better able to separate fact from opinion, substance from rhetoric and become better consumers of information in our media-centered culture.

This volume of the Opposing Viewpoints Series does not advocate a particular point of view. Quite the contrary! The very nature of the book leaves it to the reader to formulate the opinions he or she finds most suitable. My purpose as publisher is to see that this is made possible by offering a wide range of viewpoints which are fairly presented.

David L. Bender
Publisher

Introduction

"Censorship ends in logical completeness when nobody is allowed to read any books except the books nobody can read."

George Bernard Shaw

In 443 BC, the Comitia Centuriata, one of the ruling bodies of the ancient Roman State, established the office of censor. Originally, the censor was charged with taking a census of all Roman citizens for purposes of taxation, voting, and military service. In time, however, the power and authority of the censor grew until eventually the person holding the office became the official arbiter of Roman manners and morals. All Roman citizens, both commoner and aristocrat, might be permanently relieved of their civil rights for actions which the censor declared inconsistent with Rome's moral standards. The authoritarian arm of the censor could not be checked by station or influence. It reached even into the hallowed chambers of the powerful Roman Senate as certain senators found themselves removed from office, publicly ostracized and often banished from their beloved city.

Historically, the Roman Censor was not unique. The censorship of peoples, either officially or unofficially, is represented by a long, unbroken thread which traces to antiquity. From the death sentence handed the Greek philosopher Socrates for allegedly corrupting the youth of ancient Athens to the countless attempts by modern local and national governments to restrict access to both public and private information, the shadow of censorship can be seen. And significantly, censorship is not the exclusive domain of governments and societies notorious for their reactionary and oppressive policies. The censor can even be found where benevolence reigns.

This question remains: Why is censorship such a pervasive element in human history? Perhaps the answer might be that censorship, whether associated with institutions or individuals and whether involving ideas or objects, appears to be consistent with certain universal behavioral traits in humans. These traits reveal that most, if not all, people strive for conformity and differ only in the degree of their commitment to it. As distasteful as

13

the realization may seem to many, conformity often is pursued with such unrelenting zeal that it almost gives the appearance of being an innate part of the human condition. Moreover, attempts to maintain conformity are manifest at virtually all levels of human enterprise — in families, organizations, churches, and nations. A Catholic does not teach his child the precepts of the Islamic faith. A nation will not permit a group of citizens to adhere to one set of laws while allowing another group to exist unencumbered by those same laws.

One does not have to magnify the definition of conformity to uncover the relationship between it and censorship. To say "conform to that which I believe is right" is equivalent to saying "avoid that which I believe is wrong." It logically follows that "wrong" behavioral traits or attitudes will be censored, "right" ones will be rewarded. The undeniable fact is that every human being, from infancy, is taught to adhere to codes of behavior which conform to parental and community standards. And as learning results from observation and example, virtually all of humanity has been subtly nurtured in the art of censorship.

This anthology of opposing viewpoints does not attempt to uncover the psychological or physiological cradles of censorship. Rather, it presents what the editor believes are those concrete and often complex censorship issues which affect the individual, the local community, and the nation. The topics debated include: Should There Be Limits to Free Speech? Should the Press Be Regulated? Does National Security Justify Censorship? Is School and Library Censorship Justified? and Should Erotic Materials Be Censored? As the reader sifts through what will often be passionate and contentious debates, he or she should be mindful of a certain truism: The human intellect is limited both in its capacity for knowledge and its perceptions of knowledge. Even things which seem apparent — a robust wine, a lyrical melody, fragrant jasmine — are transformed by the subjective experiences of the observer. Emma Goldman, the famous Russian-born anarchist, perhaps best captured this thought in her essay, "What I Believe." After a lifetime of being censored for her radicalism, she wrote that human ideas and institutions are human constructions and therefore subject to human error. No one possesses a monopoly on truth and therefore no one holds the right to dictate morals and mores to others. "What I believe is a process rather than a finality. Finalities," she concluded ironically, "are for governments, not for the human intellect."

Should There Be Limits to Free Speech?

Chapter Preface

Should there be limits to free speech? Many Americans would answer *No* to this question. Freedom of expression is one of the basic privileges bestowed on all Americans by the Bill of Rights, the first ten Amendments to the Constitution. Traditionally, no form of expression should be censored unless it poses a direct harm to others.

But the question inevitably arises regarding the kinds of harm from which people should be protected—from racists who preach hatred and foment violence? from anarchists who advocate an end to legitimate government? from people or organizations which promote harmful products or which vividly portray sex or violence in the public media?

While some Americans believe the public should be protected from all of these things, others say that such protections are merely forms of censorship. Preventing an anarchist from preaching revolution is one step toward censoring *all* unpopular kinds of expression.

The viewpoints in this chapter debate three topics revolving around the issue of protection vs. censorship. By considering these viewpoints, the reader may come closer to an answer to the questions *should* there be limits to free speech, and, if so, what kinds of limits?

"A society that hates racism would not permit it to flourish."

Speech Should Be Limited

Rod Davis

In July 1983, *The Progressive,* a liberal magazine adamantly in favor of free expression, opened its pages to a debate about whether or not all forms of expression should be protected. The two writers argue whether groups such as the Ku Klux Klan, an openly racist organization, should be allowed to disseminate their views. Excerpts from both sides of the debate are included in this chapter. The first writer, Rod Davis, is the former editor of *The Texas Observer* and a teacher of English at the University of Texas. In the following viewpoint, Mr. Davis claims that a country's values are reflected by its policies. If a country does not believe in racism, it should not protect racist expression.

As you read, consider the following questions:

1. What evidence does Mr. Davis give of the Klan's danger to society?
2. What does Mr. Davis mean by his statement that "free speech" is a rhetorical catchphrase . . . maintained by governments to fetishize concepts routinely abrogated in practice"?
3. What does Mr. Davis think should be done about groups such as the Klan?

Rod Davis, "Free Speech for the Klan Is a Fraud, Not a Right," *The Progressive,* July 1983. Reprinted by permission from *The Progressive,* 409 East Main Street, Madison, WI 53703. Copyright © 1984, The Progressive, Inc.

What should be done to prevent the resurgence of the Ku Klux Klan in the United States? Everything possible, by broadbased, organized, enthusiastic popular opposition. Whether or not the Government certifies such action through various facades of "legality" is irrelevant, just as official approval of mass action has been irrelevant from Mahatma Gandhi's India to Martin Luther King's America.

The issue before the Left is clear, but our line of vision must not wander. We must not be concerned with protecting the Klan from the abstract encroachments of governmental censorship, but with protecting the people—including all nonwhites and non-Protestants in this instance—from the real, documentable, historical violence of the Klan and its allies.

For more than 120 years, the Klan has murdered and organized, first in the South and later in the volatile racist North and East. Now it is organizing in the West as well: Marin County, California, has an active Klan which harasses the few black residents, and in Oregon the Klan has found a hate-wedge by recruiting against hippies and Orientals. . . .

Though estimates of current membership vary—the number is probably around 20,000, based on projections from a 1981 *New York Times* report—it is fair to guess that the Klan renaissance is significant.

Klan Infestation

The revival encompasses violent attacks, paramilitary camps, bookstores, frequent public and media appearances, and renewed perception of Klan strength at the community level. In my state, Texas, the Klan has run a media blitz this year with city council-approved rallies in three major cities, and in rural east Texas there is a virtual epidemic of Klan support. In Alabama, Georgia, the Carolinas, Michigan, Maryland, the Klan is a reality —an active malignant presence with an impact that reaches far beyond the firelight circle of white-robed racists and black-uniformed storm troopers. In some cases—for example, in Greensboro, North Carolina—the Klan has infested the law enforcement and judicial systems that are supposed to control it.

Is there any reason for society, and especially for the Left, not to oppose the Klan and the racism of which it is merely the ugly symbol with a ferocity equal to that mustered against the Vietnam war, segregation, the draft, child abuse, and sexism? Incredibly, there is a preferred reason. It is suggested that instead of *opposing* the Klan and racism, we ought to *defend* the Klan and the larger issue of "free speech."

This is absurd, it is insulting, and, insofar as it places the rituals of an arbitrary government above the real need for protection of the non-WASP citizenry, it is racist. "Free speech." What rhetorical catchphrase is in greater need of deconstruc-

'Watsa matter, don't you like freedom of speech?'

Ollie Harrington, Daily World.

tion? ''Free speech,'' unlike racial terror, is an abstraction, and abstractions are maintained by governments to fetishize concepts routinely abrogated in practice.

If free speech means anything, it can only refer to the expression of a hazy range of interpretations within the ideological parameters of an enforcing power. The ''free speech'' of the dominant class will never be the free speech of the oppressed and exploited, and saying so in the face of historical experience is dissembling. . . .

19

Government caprice regarding free speech is notorious. Were Japanese-Americans accorded free speech in their internment camps? Did the Smith Act, the Dred Scott decision, the recent CIA regulations provide unfettered dialogue for their respective targets? Are we supposed to wait for the Government to grant or withdraw permission to discuss social change? Did the Southern civil rights movement wait on the mighty shield of the First Amendment or just sit in those buses and at those lunch counters, and die in bullet-riddled cars?

What *is* this phantom? Just as some white-dominated city councils were giving the Klan "free speech" permits to rally last spring, another governmental body, the State Department, denied an entry visa to Salvador Allende's widow because her scheduled speech to church groups in California was deemed "prejudicial to U.S. interests." That is, the Government tagged her as a communist.

Constitutional "free speech," in the daily, concrete world, consists of what the Government decides it to be. It is a fantasy to insist that in protecting our enemies we protect ourselves. We are already under attack. FBI guidelines implemented in March go so far as to equate political activism (including union membership) with organized crime as a proper focus for Federal scrutiny.

Play us no Nero violins of "free speech" while the Left is being systematically burned. Defending the Klan's "right" to appear publicly defends nothing more than the Klan, in the same way that pursuing peace with honor meant nothing more than pursuing war. As for "free speech" outside relations to the Government—who would claim there is free speech on the shop floor, in church, at school, or in the media?

Defeat of Racism

Stop the Klan, for it is not the grotesqueries of the Klan mentality which are being opposed but the acceptability of the Klan within its white host. If you feel that the defeat of racism is a greater priority to society than is continued worship of the legal fiction of "free speech," then you see the issue clearly. And you will not subscribe to the secondary liberal position that demonstrating against the Klan means "stooping to the Klan's level." One does not stoop to the level of an enemy by opposing it; the millions who fought and died in the war against Hitler so testify. . . .

A society creates itself—its tools, its language, its ideas. It is the responsibility of society to produce that which will reflect its values. A society that hates racism would not permit it to flourish and would, in particular, not allow a vanguard racist group to operate with official sanction and police protection.

That our society does afford sanction is but a statement that we will employ anything, even the phantom fetish of the First Amendment, to let racism persist. The need actively to oppose the Klan, denying it any vestige of protection, is paramount. If you waver behind the mirage of "free speech," you must consider the possibility of complicity.

Right to Protection

There is no question that the First Amendment guarantees our right to free speech without fear, but does that right include the right to advocate hate and threats to harass and kill those whom we do not like? Why should the KKK have the privilege to incite its members to kill Jews, "Niggers," homosexuals?

After John Hinckley's attempt to assassinate Ronald Reagan, a huge protective shield was set up to guard the President. Blacks, Jews, and others feel they have the same right to protection from a group that openly advocates hate, violence, and death.

May Goldman, letter in *The Progressive*, August 1983.

If, on the other hand, you believe that "freedom" and "speech" are products of social interaction, not black-robed writ, and that a society which produces racist and fascist sects cannot possibly mean anything when it boasts "free speech," then you will have no more compunction about shutting out the Klan than a doctor would about injecting against smallpox.

Action against the Klan is a statement, long overdue, about the depth of our perception about race—a perception which must not be diluted by rational-sounding, legalistic discourse. This statement should not be left to fringe crazies; no tiny group should co-opt the obligation of society to resolve what is our greatest historical social disease. Even Woody Allen, nobody's casual thug, observed that the only way to deal with the Nazis and the Klan is with baseball bats. Especially the early, wooden ones.

"If any group can be denied the most fundamental of liberties . . . then no group is safe."

Speech Should Not Be Limited

Nat Hentoff

Nat Hentoff is the second writer in the *Progressive* debate on freedom of expression (see previous viewpoint). Mr. Hentoff, whose writings are frequently found in liberal publications, has been a board member for the American Civil Liberties Union. His views on the First Amendment can also be found in his book *The First Freedom: The Tumultuous History of Free Speech in America.* In the following viewpoint, Mr. Hentoff insists that all forms of expression, whether or not they are agreeable, must be allowed in a free society.

As you read, consider the following questions:

1. Although many people consider the ideas of organizations such as the Ku Klux Klan to be dangerous, Nat Hentoff does not believe this justifies silencing them. Why?
2. What does Mr. Hentoff mean when he says that the First Amendment "is indivisible"?
3. What is the "heckler's veto"? What does Mr. Hentoff think about it?

Nat Hentoff, "If the Klan Can Be Gagged, None of Us Is Safe," *The Progressive*, July 1983. Reprinted by permission from *The Progressive*, 409 East Main Street, Madison, WI 53703.

Reading Rod Davis's lyrical tribute to Thomas Hobbes's "state of nature," I had the sense of having heard similar cadences of righteousness, similar bold, brave solutions to national evils. And then I remembered the passage:

"We had the moral right, we had the duty to our people, to kill this people that wanted to kill us. . . . By and large we can say that we have performed this task in love of our people. And we have suffered no damage from it in our inner self, in our soul, in our character."

That reflective chord was sounded by Heinrich Himmler. It fits right into Davis's piece because Davis's thinking in this matter is totalitarian. The Klan is dangerous, and worse. Therefore, the Klan must be smashed. By whom? Well, you can't trust the Government to do it. That part of Government that has not been infiltrated by the Klan is hung up on the artificial, ritualistic, racist, classist, utterly bourgeois First Amendment.

So who will smash the Klan? Those with the will and the power and the requisite scorn for such irrelevant niceties as the law, let alone the Bill of Rights. As Huey Long said, if fascism comes to America, it will be in the guise of antifascism.

Bigger Sticks

Let us begin where Davis does. If, as he says, legality is "irrelevant," then I assume that Davis himself, sustaining the integrity of his beliefs, will never come to the ACLU or any other civil-liberties organization for aid if *his* rights to speak and demonstrate are staved in with a pole or an axe. If he survives, he'll just pick up a bigger pole or axe or dynamite charge. That's what I meant about Davis summoning us back to a "state of nature." The survival of the best armed. . . .

The purpose, by the way, of most mass action—Davis, not incidentally, omits the word "nonviolent" in characterizing the mass action of Gandhi and Martin Luther King—has been to *change* the legal system. Or to make it do what it says. Neither Gandhi nor King nor even the Wobblies found the legal system irrelevant. Legal systems gave these mass actions specific focus. The Wobblies, for instance, conducted their grand free-speech fights (nonviolent) in the streets of cities in the West because they considered the First Amendment so palpable they used it as a weapon.

As for the bloody, vicious history of the Klan, and its current resurgence, even a rotting police force can be—and has been—forced to bust Klan members for criminal activity, forced by civil-liberties and civil-rights lawyers who have a good deal more courage and stamina in these matters than folks who get their jollies (and their rush of virtue) by throwing stones at Klan marchers.

23

Such lawyers oppose the Klan with "ferocity," to use Davis's term, but they are far too concerned with *everyone's* liberties to deny the Klan the right to such noncriminal activities as speaking, writing, and assembling. When they defend the Klan on those grounds, they are defending us all, and that's why they do it.

Oppression Multiplies

This notion, Davis tells us, is absurd, insulting, racist, abstract. Well, again, let's look at the alternative in the nonabstract society. If any group can be denied the most fundamental of liberties —because if you can't speak and write, you can't change a damned thing—then no group is safe. If Davis's countervigilantes get enough numbers and weapons to suppress the Klan in a particular city, then his truth squad can go on to shut down other dangers to the motherland. Native Nazis, for one. And how about members of Phyllis Schlafly's Eagle Forum? How about anybody organized on the basis of sexism, anti-affirmative action, or whatever else is dangerous to the people's welfare? How about, ultimately, critics of Rod Davis?

An Open Society

The policy of our government must always tilt in the direction of free speech.

Why? Not because we like a speaker or agree with his views, but because America is an open society. By shouting down or locking out other voices, we damage ourselves—and become like the societies we must be free to oppose.

Editorial, *USA Today*, May 4, 1983.

If the law is irrelevant, if the First Amendment is abstract, what is to stop the Davis truth squad and, on the other hand, those who will surely rise to do battle with it? Since Davis and his allies are all true populists who simply want to purge the nation of inferior people, maybe the answer is for us just to have faith that he will do only good, and smite the doers of evil. Are any of you willing to take that leap into faith? . . .

I rather think it's too late, but before he orders the denim uniforms, Davis might look at some First Amendment history in view of his notion that only the "dominant class" gets to exercise free speech. Maybe he doesn't think kids count, but the Supreme Court's decision in *Tinker v. Des Moines Independent School District* (1969) has given students all over the country personal knowledge of the First Amendment through free-press battles they've won. And those kids are hardly all from the "dominant class.''

But look at the conscientious objectors during the Vietnam war, and what the First Amendment did to broaden the grounds for exemption. And indeed, look at the First Amendment battles, a good many of them won, by Martin Luther King and other civil-rights marchers and demonstrators in the civil-rights campaigns. The court victories achieved by them applied to everybody because—and this point eludes Davis—the First Amendment is indivisible.

An example: Last October, in Texas City, Texas, the cops arrested four Klan members and charged them with the crime of ''unlawful handbilling.'' Nobody can distribute leaflets in Texas City without first getting a permit. And the city commission has absolute discretion to decide who can march and speak and who can't.

First Amendment for All.

The Klansmen went right to the Greater Houston ACLU. Stefan Presser, the ACLU staff counsel, despises the Klan at least as much as Rod Davis does. But unlike Davis, he knows how the First Amendment actually works. Presser reminded Texas City officials that the Supreme Court ruled in 1969 that no government has the right to stop anyone from leafleting and speaking on the ground that he hasn't obtained official permission to do so. That 1969 case, Presser told his Klan clients, had been brought against the city of Birmingham, Alabama, by the Reverend Fred Shuttlesworth, an ally of Martin Luther King and one of the bravest of all the civil-rights activists in the South. Texas City is now going to scrap its licensing requirement, and now everybody is going to be able to speak in the streets there without interference. Everybody. Including Rod Davis and his gang. That's what I mean by the First Amendment being indivisible.

What would Davis prefer? That the Klan still not be allowed to parade in Texas City and that the city commission still be able to stifle whomever it wants? He can't have it both ways. If there is to be no licensing, everyone must be able to speak. Including the Klan. . . .

I would be remiss in my devotion to that phantom fetish, the First Amendment, if I did not also point out another difficulty with Rod Davis's plan to silence the Klan forevermore. I mean the ''heckler's veto.'' If a Klan demonstration is not protected by the First Amendment—that is, if the State is not prepared to extend physical protection to those who would express profoundly unpopular ideas—then the Davises who threaten or actually commit violence have successfully exercised the ''heckler's veto.'' They have decided who shall not be heard—even if there are those at the demonstration who would like to hear, for

Reprinted with permission.

whatever reason, what those racists have to say.

A small matter, Rod Davis would say. Certain people should simply not be heard, no matter who *wants* to hear them. And if people who want to hear Klan speakers don't shut up, in the new society, the new FBI will start keeping tabs on them because they are obviously a danger to the purity of the State.

Back in 1961, a lot of people with ferocious ideals similar to those of Rod Davis wanted to prevent George Lincoln Rockwell, the American Nazi leader, from speaking in a New York City park. The ACLU took the case and a judge, overturning a lower-court decision denying Rockwell the right to talk, said:

"The unpopularity of views, their shocking quality, their obnoxiousness, and even their alarming impact is not enough [to prohibit speech]. Otherwise, the preacher of any strange doctrine could be stopped; the anti-racist himself could be suppressed if he undertakes to speak in 'restricted' areas; and one who asks that public schools be open indiscriminately to all ethnic groups could be lawfully suppressed, if only he chose to speak where persuasion is needed most."

It's lucky for that judge he doesn't live in Texas. Some antifascist might bounce a rock off his skull.

"The evidence that TV violence has a harmful effect on normal viewers [is] 'overwhelming.'"

Dramatized Violence Should Be Censored

National Coalition on Television Violence

The question of harm caused by the depiction of violence on television, in movies, and in other mass media is frequently debated. The National Coalition on Television Violence (NCTV) was formed to try to drastically reduce such depiction. In the following viewpoint, the organization describes conclusions drawn from research and suggests ways to reduce the portrayal of violence.

As you read, consider the following questions:

1. List several of the authorities the NCTV cites to support the harmfulness of televised violence.
2. What reasons does Dr. Radecki, chairman of NCTV, give for lack of Congressional action?
3. What does Dr. Radecki suggest as a method to eliminate much televised violence?
4. Some psychologists believe that dramatized violence is cathartic, that by viewing it, people lose the need to act it out. How does Dr. Radecki respond to this idea?

"TV Violence Increased to Record Levels," press release, November 9, 1984 by the National Coalition on Television Violence, 1530 P Street NW, Washington, DC 20005.

Prime-time television violence has reached a new high according to the National Coalition on Television Violence. The increase is the fourth year in a row according to the NCTV monitoring results. In 1980, "Dukes of Hazzard" was the second most violent program on television with 18 acts of violence per hour. Today, it still has 18 acts of violence per hour, but now 20 programs are more violent. . . .

NCTV reports that TV violence has increased by 65% since 1980 when research was already documenting solid evidence of harm. NCTV notes that the Surgeon General and the National Institute of Mental Health concluded in 1982 that the evidence that TV violence has a harmful effect on normal viewers was "overwhelming." The U.S. Dept. of Justice report in 1983 concluded that virtually 100% of aggression researchers agree that there is a cause-effect relationship between the consumption of entertainment violence and an increased tendency towards anger and violence in viewers. The U.S. Attorney General's Task Force on Family Violence reported earlier this year that the evidence is becoming "overwhelming" that TV violence is playing a significant role in the high levels of violence in the American family.

NCTV is encouraging citizens to pressure both government and sponsors for immediate action. . . .

NCTV's chairman, Dr. Thomas Radecki, a psychiatrist with the University of Illinois School of Medicine, . . . was asked who was responsible for the high levels of violence. He said, "I think that we are all responsible for allowing this intense promotion of a barbaric and almost neo-Nazi ethic. But the American people are not being given the honest information from the Surgeon General, the American Medical Association, and the aggression research community. . . .

Broadcasters Promote Violence

TV broadcasters promote violent entertainment almost every hour on public airwaves in spite of being given free licenses to use those airwaves as long as they use them in the public interest. We estimate that the average viewer will see 2000 advertisements each year promoting violent programs and almost never hear the warning that the Surgeon General has determined that TV violence is unconsciously harmful to normal children and normal adult viewers. Instead of taking away their licenses to broadcast, some in Congress are trying to "deregulate" television, virtually giving away the public airwaves to the violent TV industry."

Dr. John Murray of Boystown submitted NCTV's counter-advertising proposal to the U.S. Senate subcommittee hearings. The proposed legislation would require that for every 3 advertisements promoting entertainment violence, that one free advertising slot would be given to citizens or citizen groups to get the message of the Surgeon General out to viewers. This same approach was very effective in cigarette counteradvertising in 1967-1970 on television. Radecki said, "I have confidence that, if the American people are only informed about the truth of how they are unconsciously learning values of anger and violence, that they will turn the channel. The continued one-sided promotion of violent entertainment by NBC, CBS, and ABC is false and deceptive advertising of the most dangerous variety. The American people have a right to honest information."

Dr. Radecki was asked why Congress and the White House

© Pierott/Rothco

had not done anything if the information was so conclusive. He said, "It is clear to me that one factor is that the TV and movie industry has bought powerful influence in the U.S. Congress. In the just past election, the entertainment industry is on record as giving over $1,500,000 to selected congressmen who sit on the very committees that decide these issues."

Indefensible Entertainment

Dr. Radecki even placed some of the blame on American churches and educational institutions. "In spite of the overwhelming evidence, relatively few churches or schools have a regular program of informing their members or students of the seriousness of this issue and of which programs are high in entertainment violence from which both children and adults should abstain. It is both medically unhealthy and morally indefensible for anyone to entertain him or herself with violence. Just last week I spoke at a Catholic high school where 75% of the student body had seen *Friday the 13th.* Another 20% had seen *Texas Chainsaw Massacre.* And yet, the theater versions of these movies have been proven to cause significant increases in the willingness to rape women in normal college males. A significant number of Lutheran women in a concerned group of mothers to which I spoke had seen movies of intense violence, not realizing that research clearly shows harmful effects on normal adults as well as children.

"Churches and schools in our nation need to get this information out to the public, especially when our government is failing so miserably. A number of church magazines and newsletters have begun to carry our research information. We must put pressure on the advertisers and threaten to boycott GM and Chrysler cars, give up R.J. Reynolds cigarettes and Kentucky Fried Chicken. We must especially let our Congressional representatives know that it is not right for the government to underwrite large amounts of TV violence."

Asked whether a boycott would work, Dr. Radecki replied, "I am sure it will if churches, schools, and citizen groups get out the information. In 1983, we suggested a boycott of Saturday morning cartoon sponsors and we have gotten improvement two years in a row on Saturday morning. Researchers and advertisers have been meeting." . . .

Disproven Catharsis Theory

Dr. Radecki was challenged by a reporter who noted that Dr. Jib Fowles, a researcher from the University of Houston had testified to the U.S. Congress that TV violence was a good way to relieve tension. Radecki replied, . . . "Fowles has never done a single psychological or aggression research study in his life.

Fowles is simply a well-intentioned, but seriously misinformed humanities professor from Texas who likes violent programming. No aggression researcher alive today supports the long-disproven catharsis theory. Violence begets violence, not relieves it. For the wire services and networks to present Fowles as a researcher is a sad misrepresentation to the American people."

"The... community should go beyond the counting of swear words or acts of violence on screen, and ask instead what point of view is displayed in a particular work."

Common Sense, Not Censorship, Should Regulate Drama

James M. Wall

James M. Wall, managing editor of *The Christian Century* magazine, is project chairman of the National Council of Churches' Project on Pornography. Like many people, he is concerned about the influence of the mass media on society. In the following viewpoint, Mr. Wall points out that many depictions of violence are sensitive, honest portrayals of painful subject matter. He believes that cooperation between media producers and the public can encourage such portrayals and discourage exploitative depictions.

As you read, consider the following questions:

1. Mr. Wall opens his viewpoint with an example of a rape scene taken from a television program. Why does he think this type of scene is acceptable while others may not be?
2. Mr. Wall states that "a society is sometimes forced to save individuals from themselves" through such devices as censorship. Does he want to see this happen to forestall "media pollution"?

James M. Wall, "Point of View Shapes Media Sex and Violence," Copyright 1985 Christian Century Foundation. Reprinted by permission from the February 6-13, 1985 issue of The Christian Century.

A nurse leaves the hospital after working the night shift. In the dark parking lot, she attempts to start her car. After several efforts she still can't get the engine to turn over. Suddenly a man appears at the car window and offers to help. She declines nervously, and again turns the ignition key. But the man returns, this time smashing the car window.

That scene from the television production St. Elsewhere depicts the beginning of a brutal rape. But the physical attack itself is not shown. After the window breaks, the film cuts to another scene, developing a different subplot. It is not until several scenes later that the nurse reappears. Gently coaxed by a hospital social worker, the victim describes what took place after the window was broken. It is a painful restatement of a traumatic moment, described entirely from the nurse's point of view.

Victim's Experience

In contrast to depictions of sexual violence in many other films and television shows, the St. Elsewhere creative team chose to focus audience attention on what the experience meant to the victim. It is not pleasant, but it is an honest portrayal, sensitively presented. That television episode was shown here to a panel representing the National Council of Churches (NCC) during a two-day hearing on sex and violence in the media.

Steve Bello, one of the writers of the assault episode, testified before the panel during the hearings. He showed the TV clip to make his point that no limitations should be placed on media subject matter. Bello was one of 16 witnesses, drawn largely from the motion picture and television industries, appearing before the NCC panel in the second of three national hearings. The third will focus on possible legislative remedies for the growing emphasis on exploitative sex and gratuitous violence in the media.

St. Elsewhere and Hill Street Blues frequently were cited by both panel members and guests as television productions that traffic heavily in sexual and violent materials, but that do so with respect for the persons involved. In chairing these hearings I was reminded again that a key phrase in judging any fictional treatment is "point of view." In script development, that term means that a scene is shot from the viewpoint of a particular participant in the action. In the St. Elsewhere episode, the use of the nurse's point of view rather than that of her attacker entirely removed any suggestion of sexual feeling. In many of the sleazy "slasher" films (for example, the *Friday the 13th* series) the point of view shifts between that of the victim (terror) and that of the victimizer (lust).

A film's perspective determines audience reaction. Sharing the experience of an assault victim, the viewer feels the help-

"THERE IS NOTHING WRONG WITH YOUR PICTURE...THE SHOW
YOU ARE WATCHING IS BEING CENSORED!"

lessness, the fear and finally the rage which come from being attacked. On the other hand, the dominant emotion projected through the attacker or killer's perspective is the sense of power that comes from controlling what happens to the person subjected to violence.

Vicarious Experience?

In many sexual assault scenes the camera focuses on the victim's face, requiring the viewer to be in the position of the rapist. What now concerns the NCC panel and its sponsoring agency, the council's Communications Commission, is that a large number of Americans clearly want to identify with the powerful attacker in these films and television productions. This may or may not lead to imitative behavior, but it certainly offers viewers the vicarious experience of violence related to sex.

Among the producers, writers and directors who appeared here there was strong resistance to any governmental interference in the industry's creative process. But there is little evidence that the industry is prepared to avoid that interference by voluntarily governing itself. The NCC panel was also opposed to censorship as it began these hearings, but thus far it finds little indication that a middle way is emerging between total license to pollute the creative atmosphere on the one hand, and government censorship on the other.

Pollution Parallel

As one witness put it, "If people will stop paying to see this stuff, the industry will stop making it." But if one pursues the pollution parallel, which emerged in the initial New York hearing, it becomes clear that a society is sometimes forced to save individuals from themselves. Although smoking has been proven to damage health, the federal government thus far has chosen to do no more than require the tobacco companies to warn people about the danger of cancer. But laws have been implemented that require industries to clean up environmental pollution. Will warnings be enough to control media pollution, or will stronger measures be required?

The positive signs that emerged from the hearings, suggesting that industry awareness about this problem is growing, came from such witnesses as Gene Reynolds, producer of M*A*S*H and Lou Grant, two superior long-running television series. "Everything I do has a premise," Reynolds pointed out. Clearly the premise of M*A*S*H, which focused on a hospital unit at the Korean front, was antiwar, and proliving. Reynolds, most of whose shows fare well in ratings, joined other presenters in a dislike for the "bottom-line" mentality in sponsors' decision-making.

A Shift in Focus?

William Sackheim, a writer-producer involved in such films as The In-Laws, Survivors and First Blood, told a fascinating and depressing story about his experience with First Blood, starring Sylvester Stallone. Sackheim's original script focused on the premise that people who need to act out a role need role models to guide them. Stallone, who played a disturbed Vietnam veteran in the film, insisted on a shift in focus which turned the film into a tale of violence, acted out by a man trained by his country to kill. Largely lacking any redeeming purpose, First Blood made money and still plays on cable. It bears only a faint resemblance to Sackheim's original premise.

The interconnection between theatrical films like First Blood and cable television was one of the issues that led to the current hearings. Studio and independent producers insist that they make films for paying audiences who are told in advance, through the industry's classification system, what to expect. But these films eventually (sometimes within six months of their initial release) end up on major cable networks and enter homes where television sets are often controlled by small children.

Unlike adult channels, which advertise themselves as such, Home Box Office, Cinemax and Showtime offer a variety of films on cable, just one turn away from network and local programming. The innocuous promise to show R-rated films only at night merely serves as a come-on to the curious. It is this relationship between theater and home viewing that may be leading the film industry toward a federal control it wants to avoid.

Responsibility Lies with Viewer

Violence is no stranger to art and entertainment, having made its debut on the Western stage with Greek tragedy. Despite the escalation of violence in recent American movies, it seems foolish, shortsighted, and probably unconstitutional to hold the people who make these films responsible for what other people do after seeing them. The responsibility of the storyteller is to tell the story, and the responsibility for behavior lies with the individual.

Peter Koper, *American Film*, July/August 1982.

The willingness of media personnel to appear before a church panel suggests, however, that at least part of the industry is sensitive to the growing dangers both of media pollution and of censorship. Hollywood decision-makers are not automatons; they may be parents or even churchgoers. They do not operate in a vacuum. Informed protests that recognize their positive contributions as well as resist the negative are heard gratefully. The religious community should go beyond the counting of swear words or acts of violence on screen, and ask instead what point of view is displayed in a particular work. In that direction lies the possibility for cooperation between church and media.

*"A visitor from another planet. . . . might
conclude that our society had some unique set
of ethics which encouraged the selling of death,
and made it all look like fun."*

Advertising Should Be Limited

Elizabeth M. Whelan, Michael Jacobson, and George Hacker

In recent years there has been a great deal of debate as to
whether or not society needs to be protected from commercials
and advertisements that promote health-endangering products.
The authors of the following viewpoint agree with those who attack cigarette and alcohol advertisers for unethically seeking
profit at the expense of the public's health. Elizabeth M.
Whelan, author of the first part of the viewpoint, is executive
director of ACSH, the American Council on Science and Health.
The second part was written by Michael Jacobson, executive
director of the Center for Science in the Public Interest, and
George Hacker, director of the center's alcohol policies program.

As you read, consider the following questions:

1. According to Ms. Whelan, what factors make cigarette advertising an exception to the usual ideal of free speech?
2. Why do the authors of these viewpoints think that unlimited
   advertising of such things as cigarettes and alcohol actually
   prevent free speech?

Elizabeth M. Whelan, "On the Ethics of Cigarette Advertising," *ACHS News & Views*,
September/October 1984. Published by the American Council on Science and Health, 1995
Broadway, New York, NY 10023.

Michael Jacobson and George Hacker, "Ballyhooing Booze," *St. Louis Post Dispatch*,
November 18, 1984. Reprinted by permission.

I

Senator Reed Smoot (R-Utah) once described cigarette advertising as "an orgy of buncombe, quackery and downright falsehood and fraud." That was in 1930. I wonder what Senator Smoot would have to say about the tuxedoed Barclay man, the Satin businesswoman, the Marlboro macho man, the Players cocktail gala, and the Kent jock, enjoying a smoke as he towels down in the locker room.

Most of today's ads emphasize vitality with suggestions of health, outdoor activity, feminity or masculinity, success, romance, pleasure or relaxation. Young people are shown bobsledding, taking a smoke after a swim or tennis, or whooping it up at an all-American ice cream parlor. A lovely girl in a country setting invites us to "take a puff" of a Salem. A handsome man offers a Barclay to a waiting lady off camera. Young women flaunt their newly found independence in ads for Virginia Slims and More. The "man's man"—the rough and tough cowboy—shouts his supposed virility in Marlboro Country "where a man belongs." Benson and Hedges Delux 100, Sterling and others suggest a "touch of class" with accompanying pictures of caviar, champagne, silver trays, Rolls Royces, expensive sports cars, and Steinway pianos.

Incomprehensible Promotion of Death

A visitor from another planet probably could not comprehend that these ads, which total over 1.5 billion dollars in revenues each year, are promoting a product that is our nation's leading cause of premature death, accounting for over 350,000 fatalities each year.

If he was aware of these statistics, he might conclude that our society had some unique set of ethics which encouraged the selling of death, and made it all look like fun. How would you like the task of explaining to an extraterrestrial drop-in that Americans had a firm commitment to good health and therefore moved quickly to ban chemicals like EDB, which cause cancer in laboratory animals but which have never been shown to cause cancer in humans—yet the same society tolerated the promotion and sale of a product that kills some 1,000 Americans each day?

No long-necked, bulging-eyed creatures have phoned home to me yet with those questions, but a few weeks ago my six-year-old daughter, while flipping through a magazine, asked why "they" allow those ads, "when everyone knows cigarette smoking makes you sick." The simple answer, of course, is that cigarettes are a legal product and in our free society, advertising is a basic right. Cigarette companies want to promote their product; magazines want the revenue, and the transaction is as American as 100 percent natural, organic apple pie. Besides, the ads have warning labels, making it a matter of free choice; if people are stupid enough to avoid the warning, that's their tough luck.

Advertising Ethics

But is it? Isn't the cigarette phenomenon unique? Perhaps now, some twenty years after the first Surgeon General's report, confronted with some 40,000 medical and scientific references which have documented consistently the extraordinary hazards of cigarette smoking, we should give some careful consideration to the ethics of tolerating cigarette ads. Particularly we might want to re-evaluate the ethics of *misleading*—fun-filled, health-oriented—advertising of a deadly product.

Ban Harmful Ads

Action is warranted to reduce the specious appeal of alcohol to the young. Banning beer and wine ads from TV would be a good first step.

Christian Science Monitor, February 19, 1985.

My instinctive reaction to the possibility of Congress mandating an advertising ban on a legal product is negative. After all, one might argue, if government is given the cigarette inch, they will take the full regulatory mile and who knows what ads they would suppress next. But actually, faced with the task of deciding on the constitutionality of a ban on cigarette ads, the courts as well as Congress might recognize the situation for what it is: a unique problem demanding a unique solution. The ultimate legal issue might not be the right of tobacco companies to advertise, but their right to obscure health risks with *misleading* innuendo, i.e., the association of smoking with success, health, and happiness. Under those circumstances the industry might maintain its "right" to advertise but only in the form of (if you will forgive the expression) tombstone-type ads, where the hype is absent and only the bare-bones facts about the product (name, quantity, tar and nicotine levels, price, etc.) are presented, much in the same way stocks and bonds are advertised.

Cigarette Ads: A Unique Problem

A number of factors put the question of cigarette advertising in a class by itself:

First, let's recall that as a society we never made a decision to allow ads for a deadly product. The ads began some 30 years before scientific studies confirmed that cigarette smoking was life threatening.

Second, the cigarette is the only legal product available today which is harmful *when used as intended.* Alcohol, for example, must be used in abusive quantities or unacceptable circumstances (i.e., before driving) to pose a hazard. Automobiles, while a contributing factor to some 50,000 deaths every year, are reasonably safe when used appropriately.

Obviously all advertising is to some extent hyperbole—whether it is the promotion of shampoo, baby food, soda or bathing suits, the models are gorgeous and the setting is idyllic. But in these circumstances, the hyperbole in the ads does not entice consumers to purchase an inherently hazardous substance.

Third, maybe we should face up to the fact that the warning label is generally unnoticed and ineffective, and will probably continue to be so in its newer, more explicit form. The warnings tell of risk, but surveys indicate that American consumers have little knowledge of the magnitude and nature of that risk. Probably unique also is the repressive influence cigarette advertising revenues have on the free flow of negative information about cigarettes in magazines and newspapers. Whether the pressure to spike pejorative statements on smoking comes from the tobacco companies themselves or is simply perceived as pressure by editors, it is clearly there. So given the paucity of negative messages on cigarettes, relative to the omnipressent positive messages in advertising, and noting that 90 percent of smokers tell surveyors that they wish they could quit, one begins to wonder how much freedom of choice is really involved here.

II

Isn't it about time we questioned the perverted form of alcohol "education" our young receive from radio and television ads? From the age of 2 or 3, children are barraged by thousands of catchy jingles and captivating images, courtesy of the alcoholic beverage industry. These ads drum home the point that good times, success and friendships are the rewards of drinking. Such carefully crafted advertisments, along with examples set by family and peers, help mold lifelong attitudes and habits.

As kids grow older, alcoholic beverages continue to be glamorized. Virtually every imaginable form of marketing hype is tapped to get Americans, especially young people, to drink more. College newspapers and youth-oriented magazines supplement broadcast efforts. Ads ballyhoo beer as an aid to "great writing" and a substitute for study. Hundreds of student marketing representatives accelerate the flow of beer on campus. Volleyball and tennis tournaments, football and basketball games, rock music concerts and fraternity and sorority events are sponsored by alcoholic beverage producers to make drinking an integral part of the collegiate lifestyle.

With this multimedia drumbeat, is it any wonder that alcohol problems are so widespread? Despite a recent leveling, per capita alcohol consumption is up by nearly 50 percent in the past 25 years. Close to 1.5 million Americans, including 3 million under 18, have serious drinking problems. One recent study found that one of every 10 junior high and high school students in New York state was self-described as "hooked" on alcohol. According to the National Institute on Drug Abuse, an alarming 41 percent of high school seniors reported binge drinking (five or more drinks in a row) during the two weeks before the survey.

Mammoth Problem

Alcohol abuse is a mammoth problem, unrivaled in its social and economic costs to society. It is America's number one drug problem, killing well over 100,000 of us each year and costing our nation a whopping $120 billion annually in economic damage. Drinking is linked to a high percentage of violent crime. It also causes such serious health problems as cancer, birth defects and mental retardation. Perhaps most poignantly, alcohol abuse kills our young. Drunken driving is now the leading cause of death among people aged 16 to 24.

Despite the grim realities about alcohol, brewers and vintners are spending unprecedented amounts on commercials to extol the virtues of drinking. Between 1970 and 1983, expenses for radio ads shot up 300 percent, for TV ads 490 percent. Beer and wine companies now spend over $700 million a year on such advertising.

Millions of impressionable young people are exposed daily to these enticing messages. By stark contrast, public service spots about alcohol and health are the exception. When they appear they are far too often hidden in the wee hours of the morning. To help reduce the epidemic level of alcohol-related problems, a broad coalition of groups is backing a national initiative that calls for either an end to radio and television advertising for alcoholic beverages or for equal time for messages about the health and safety risks of drinking.

Groups such as the National PTA, National Council on Alcoholism and Remove Intoxicated Drivers are spearheading a petition campaign known as Project SMART (Stop Marketing Alcohol on Radio and Television). Not surprisingly, the broadcast, alcoholic beverage and advertising industries have responded by launching a counter-attack against this movement and its supporters.

Taking alcohol ads off the airways is not a panacea. This effort must be only one part of a comprehensive prevention program to help reshape our attitudes about drinking. Education programs, effective drunk driving laws, excise tax increases and improved labeling need to be considered as well.

"Censors always assume that they are strong enough to handle material that others must be shielded from."

Advertising Should Not Be Limited

Erwin Knoll and Stephen Chapman

One argument that is frequently used in censorship issues is "the public good." Many people feel that society must be protected from dangerous influences. Others, including the authors of this viewpoint, believe that everyone should have the right to make individual decisions, even if they may be unhealthy ones. Erwin Knoll, author of Part I, is the editor of *The Progressive*, a liberal monthly journal. Stephen Chapman, the author of Part II, is a nationally syndicated columnist. Together, they argue against "protective" censorship and for informed free choice.

As you read, consider the following questions:

1. Mr. Knoll states that *The Progressive* has openly denounced the tobacco industry. Yet he sees no contradiction in the magzines agreement to publish its advertising. How does he exlain this?
2. Why does Mr. Chapman believe that it would be wrong to ban alcohol advertising?
3. Do you agree with these writers when they say that the public does not need to be protected from such things as cigarette and alcohol advertising? What other kinds of ads, if any, do you think should be banned or limited?

Erwin Knoll, "Smoke Gets in Your Eyes," *The Progressive*, January 1985. Reprinted by permission from *The Progressive*, 409 East Main Street, Madison, WI 53703. Copyright © 1984, The Progressive, Inc.

Stephen Chapman, "Spare Us the Coddling," *The Washington Times*, January 29, 1985. Reprinted by permission; Tribune Media Services.

I

The caller was a *Wall Street Journal* reporter who said she was surveying several political publications. Did *The Progressive* have a policy on accepting tobacco advertising?

No, I replied, the matter had never come up: No tobacco company had tried to place an ad in *The Progressive*, and I doubted that any would.

Well, she continued, what about an institutional ad, placed in behalf of tobacco workers and urging the public to consider the unfortunate impact of antismoking regulations on the industry's employees? What would *The Progressive* do if it were offered an ad of that kind?

I thought it was a purely hypothetical question, but I did my best to answer it. We were persuaded long ago, I said, that tobacco is a toxic substance. (I'm a former three-pack-a-day smoker who quit cold turkey five years ago.) We have denounced the tobacco industry and its lobbying efforts. We've been especially critical of the Federal Government's continuing subsidies to tobacco growers and tobacco exporters.

But, I went on, we aren't censors and we don't like the censorship mentality. On the contrary, we're deeply committed to the free exchange of ideas. If the tobacco industry or its workers wanted to make a pitch to *The Progressive's* readers, I said, they could buy advertising space in this magazine at the usual rates. So long as the message did not violate the law or minimal standards of good taste, we would make room for it.

Not Hypothetical

As it turned out, the question wasn't hypothetical at all: *The Wall Street Journal's* reporter was working on a story about an advertising campaign sponsored by something called the Tobacco Industry Labor/Management Committee. The drive, funded by the Tobacco Institute, was directed particularly at publications like *The Progressive*—periodicals whose readers, it was assumed, might oppose smoking but respond favorably to a labor union appeal.

The ad is headed *"We're the Tobacco Industry, Too,"* and features a portrait of three solemn-looking individuals identified as members of the Bakery, Confectionery, and Tobacco Workers International Union Local 203T. By astonishing coincidence, one is black, one is a woman, and one is middle-aged.

Their message is summed up in the last couple of sentences of text:

"The tobacco industry creates jobs, which for many of us make the difference between poverty and dignity. It means a lot to us."

Our reaction when *The Progressive* received its copy of the ad

43

was that it amounted to a piece of cheap-shot propaganda. During the 1960s, while visiting an aerospace plant in California, I saw workers wearing buttons that read, *Don't Bite the War That Feeds You.* The tobacco ad reminded me of that shoddy episode.

But it never occurred to us to reject the ad. We assumed that some readers would be offended by the message, and members of our staff even started an office pool on how many letters of protest we would receive. It seems likely that the prize will go to someone on the high end of the pool; the mail has been heavy and is still pouring in.

Censorship Mentality

Some letters were terse—"We won't renew. Goodbye." — and others were verbose. Many asked whether *The Progressive* would publish an advertisement placed by weapons workers in defense of military spending. (The answer is yes, it would.) What intrigued me was not the criticism of the tobacco industry's message, but the insistence that *The Progressive's* readers had to be shielded from that message.

No Proof of Ad Harm

"There is absolutely no study that exists today that shows that advertising of our products contributes to the abuse of our products," says Stephen K. Lambright, vice president and group executive with responsibility for governmental affairs at Anheuser-Busch Cos. Inc., whose Budweiser beer is the nation's favorite. "There is no evidence whatsoever that an ad ban will have a meaningful effect on abusive and underage consumption."

Washington Post National Weekly Edition, December 24, 1984.

I've always had a hard time trying to understand the censorship mentality. Presumably, each of our irate correspondents had read the tobacco ad and had been left none the worse for reading it. Yet each apparently assumed that others could not be trusted to exercise such good judgment. Censors always assume that they are strong enough to handle material that others must be shielded from. Curious.

Our position is that people who subscribe to *The Progressive* are mature, intelligent, responsible human beings who can be exposed to points of view we find wrong or downright obnoxious without being led down the primrose path to perdition. Anybody want to take issue with that?

II

It has been barely a year since drinkers and other libertarians celebrated the 50th anniversary of the repeal of Prohibition.

Maybe we celebrated too soon. Ever since, people who occupy themselves by interfering with other people's private affairs have been trying to do everything short of resurrect the Volstead Act. Their latest affront is a drive to ban beer and wine ads from radio and television.

The drive is the work of a coalition of abstainers, self-styled guardians of the "public interest," and compulsive busybodies, collectively known as Project SMART (Stop Marketing Alcohol on Radio and Television). Among them: the Mormon and Baptist churches, the Center for Science in the Public Interest, and the National Parent-Teacher Association. Whatever their diversity, the groups share a stunted appreciation of personal freedom.

Still, they've collected 600,000 signatures supporting their effort to ban the ads or require broadcasters to provide free time for counterads deploring drinking. A Senate committee plans hearings.

The Safety Nazis

The safety Nazis have already gotten laws to compel seat-belt use and to ban drinking by adults under the age of 21. They got cigarette ads off the airwaves 14 years ago. But they can never rest from protecting people from the temptations of vice.

No one familiar with the history of modern social puritanism in America can be confident that drinking or smoking (or maybe even driving) will be legal half a century from now. The real Puritans would disapprove; they approved of alcohol, used sensibly. The neo-prohibitionists, by contrast, believe not only that these habits are evil, but that anything evil should be against the law.

Their latest cause is a perfect illustration. The coalition gripes that radio and TV ads glamorize drinking. No doubt they do; ads wouldn't sell much beer by convincing people it's disgusting.

But in a free society, why should it be illegal for sellers to "glamorize" legal products? Anyone who disagrees is perfectly free to propagandize against it. To silence your opponents is to admit the weakness of your case.

The coalition worries that children may be unduly influenced by these ads. Well, that's why there are laws against selling alcohol to minors. The gullibility of children is no ground for putting a straitjacket on adults. Among the pubescent, tobacco-chewing ballplayers are the best publicity chewing tobacco could get. Should we forbid telecasts showing any player with a bulge in his cheek?

Alleged Hazards

Another alleged hazard is that these ads encourage drunk driving. By that logic, auto ads are just as guilty, since they promote the other half of the drunk-driving combination. The way to

45

combat drunk driving is to enforce laws against it.

Besides defying common sense, the measure also probably violates the First Amendment. Commercial speech has always been given less protection than political speech, but this ban goes too far.

In fact, it matches the Supreme Court's description of a law it reviewed in 1976. "What is at issue," said the court, "is whether a state may completely suppress the dissemination of concededly truthful information about entirely lawful activity, fearful of that information's effect upon . . . its recipients." The court's answer: no.

Forcing broadcasters to foot the bill for "public interest" commercials ostensibly exposing the dangers of alcohol is a little more reasonable, but not much. Groups that object to drinking shouldn't expect other people to pay for the dissemination of their views. Should auto ads have to be balanced by commericals on the risks of driving? Granted, broadcasters get free use of the "public airwaves," but the obvious remedy for that defect is to charge them a fee for it.

Endless Possible Protections

There is no end to the protections that could be written into law. Why not ban commercials for eggs and ice cream as well as beer and wine? Why not ban the products themselves, along with anything else that conceivably may be dangerous?

This is an approach worthy of a nation of children who must be protected from making independent decisions lest they incur the slightest risk. It reflects the immature urge to obtain security at the expense of liberty, including the liberty of those who disagree.

Distinguishing Between Fact and Opinion

This activity is designed to help develop the basic reading and thinking skill of distinguishing between fact and opinion. Consider the following statement as an example: "Careful monitoring of television programs shows that since 1980 depiction of violence has increased nearly 100 percent." This statement is a fact with which few people who have looked at the research could disagree. But consider another statement about television violence: "Television violence harms all of us as is shown by the rising national crime rate." The connection between television violence and the national crime rate is arguable and this statement includes nothing to factually connect the two.

When investigating controversial issues it is important that one be able to distinguish between statements of fact and statements of opinion. It is also important to recognize that not all statements of fact are true. They may appear to be true, but some are based on inaccurate or false information. For this activity, however, we are concerned with understanding the difference between those statements which appear to be factual and those which appear to be based primarily on opinion.

Most of the following statements are taken from the viewpoints in this chapter. Consider each statement carefully. *Mark O for any statement you believe is an opinion or interpretation of facts. Mark F for any statement you believe is a fact.*

If you are doing this activity as a member of a class or group, compare your answers with those of other class or group members. Be able to defend your answers. You may discover that others will come to different conclusions than you. Listening to the reasons others present for their answers may give you valuable insights in distinguishing between fact and opinion.

If you are reading this book alone, ask others if they agree with your answers. You too will find this interaction very valuable.

> *O = opinion*
> *F = fact*

f 1. The current membership of the Ku Klux Klan is about 20,000.

2. The renaissance of the Ku Klux Klan is significant.

3. The "free speech" of the dominant class will never be the free speech of the oppressed and exploited classes.

4. Constitutional "free speech" consists of what the government decides it to be.

5. A society that hates racism would not permit it to flourish in the name of free speech.

f 6. Last October, in Texas City, Texas, the police arrested four Klan members and charged them with the crime of "unlawful handbilling."

7. Regardless of our concept of free speech, certain people should simply not be heard, no matter who wants to hear them.

f 8. Virtually 100% of aggression researchers agree that there is a cause-effect relationship between the consumption of entertainment violence and an increased tendency toward anger and violence in viewers.

9. We estimate that the average viewer will see 2000 advertisements each year promoting violent programs.

10. The American people have a right to honest information.

11. It is both medically unhealthy and morally indefensible for anyone to entertain him or herself with violence.

12. *St. Elsewhere* and *Hill Street Blues* are television shows that traffic in sexual and violent materials, but that do so with respect for the persons involved.

13. The cable television promise to show R-rated films only at night merely serves as a come-on to the curious.

14. Hollywood decision-makers are not automatons; they may be parents or even churchgoers.

15. Most of today's cigarette ads emphasize vitality with suggestions of health, outdoor activity, feminity or masculinity, success, romance, pleasure, or relaxation.

16. Cigarette ads, which total over 1.5 billion dollars in revenues each year, are promoting a product that is our nation's leading cause of premature death, accounting for over 350,000 fatalities each year.

17. Maybe we should face up to the fact that the cigarette warning label is generally unnoticed and ineffective.

18. Drinking is linked to a high percentage of violent crime.

Periodical Bibliography

The following list of periodical articles deals with the subject matter of this chapter.

Morris G. Abram "What Constitutes a Civil Right?" *The New York Times Magazine*, June 10, 1984.

America "The Rights of Bigotry," June 18, 1983.

David Brock "The Big Chill," *Policy Review*, Spring 1985.

William O. Douglas "A Justice's Case for Free Speech," *Liberty*, July/August 1977.

Art Goldberg "Right to Heckle," *The Nation*, April 2, 1983.

Janet Guyon "Do Publications Avoid Anti-Cigarette Stories to Protect Ad Dollars?" *The Wall Street Journal*, November 22, 1982.

Virginia Held "Free Expression," *Society*, September/October 1984.

Nat Hentoff "The Principals of Censorship," *The Progressive*, May 1984.

Peter Koper "Can Movies Kill?" *American Film*, July/August 1982.

Lance Morrow "Holding the Speaker Hostage," *Time*, April 11, 1983.

The New England Journal of Medicine "Cigarette Advertising and Media Coverage of Smoking and Health," February 7, 1985.

Kenneth W. Roberts "Are Liberals Really Devoted to Free Speech?" *New Guard*, Winter 1982-83.

The Tobacco Institute "Peer Pressure and Acting "Grown Up"—the Big Reasons Youngsters Smoke," Available from *The Tobacco Institute*, 1875 I Street NW, Washington, DC 20006.

U.S. News & World Report "What Is TV Doing to America?" August 2, 1982.

Larry White "Total Ban on Cigarette Advertising: Is It Constitutional?" *ACHS News & Views*, September/October 1984. Available from *The American Council on Science and Health*, 1995 Broadway, New York, NY 10023.

Should the News Media Be Regulated?

Chapter Preface

Although journalists are protected by the First Amendment's "freedom of the press" clause, critics complain that reporters seem to believe that getting a story is more important than anything else—personal privacy, national security, even truth. In order to "scoop" their competition, the critics say, journalists sometimes jump to conclusions or accept unquestioningly "facts" that have not been verified.

One area of strong concern is in cases of personal and corporate reputation. If a person or corporation believes that a journalist has distorted the truth or told damaging lies, it can sue the journalist or the publisher for libel. Prior to 1964, journalists were sometimes sued for damaging a reputation even if what the journalist wrote might have been true. But in the 1964 landmark case, New York Times v. Sullivan, the Supreme Court ruled that it was not enough for a person (or company) to *feel* maligned. It must be proved that the journalist wrote or broadcast material that he or she *knew* was false or that he or she did not bother to verify. This ruling offered strong protection to investigative reporters and other journalists who may have been inhibited from writing important stories for fear of being brought into court. Many journalists feel that with the passage of time, the impact of the New York Times v. Sullivan ruling has eroded, putting journalists once again at the mercy of a sue-happy population.

In addition to the problem of libel, this chapter deals with whether or not journalists can—or should—be trusted with sensitive government information and whether or not the kinds of materials broadcast by radio and television should be regulated.

"Given the media's record in recent years, it would have been suicidal to confide in any of the reporters who cover the White House and the Pentagon."

The Press Should Be Barred from Secret Military Maneuvers

Ralph de Toledano

In October 1983, the United States Marines invaded the tiny, politically troubled Caribbean island of Grenada with the stated intent of removing to safety the American citizens living there. For the first time, the US media were not only not allowed to accompany the US force but were not informed of the planned invasion. In the following viewpoint, Ralph de Toledano, a conservative syndicated columnist, explains why he believes the government was right in excluding the press.

As you read, consider the following questions:

1. Mr. de Toledano states that the media's attitude toward secrecy and security are different today than in the past. What change does he observe?
2. Mr. de Toledano says that "the Fourth Estate [journalists] now acts as if it were the fourth arm of government." What does he mean?
3. Why does Mr. de Toledano believe that the First Amendment was *not* violated in this instance?

Ralph de Toledano, "Grenada and the Press," *The Union Leader*, November 11, 1983. Reprinted by permission.

Ever since the invasion of Grenada the press has been, as the saying goes, waxing wroth because it was not given advance notice by the White House or the Pentagon. And Larry Speakes, President Reagan's press secretary has, it is rumored, threatened to resign because he was not informed of the plans for the military operation. These complaints have been given page 1 prominence by the *Washington Post.*

It is needless to point out that the White House and the Pentagon were wise in keeping the media at arm's length. The operation, if it was to complete its mission of rescuing the 1,000 Americans on the Communist-controlled island, required two elements: *secrecy and surprise.* If so much as a hint of the landings had reached the Grenadian military junta, there could have been a slaughter of the innocent. At the very least they would have been held hostage with all the horror that entails, as we learned in Iran.

Reporter's Unbuttoned Lips

Once upon a time, it is true, the press could have been trusted to keep its lip buttoned. But given the media's record in recent years, it would have been suicidal to confide in any of the reporters who cover the White House and the Pentagon. They would have clamored for details of time and place—and you may be sure that some of the more zealous among them would have charged up Capitol Hill to get the comments of members of the House and Senate Armed Services committees.

To brief the press before U.S. forces had made contact with the Grenadian and Cuban troops on the island would have been tantamount to announcing the imminent operation on TV evening news. As to Speakes, he would have come under sharp and vicious attack from the White House press corps when it became known that he shared the vital secret but had not leaked it to the media prima donnas. Now he can say, "Boys, how could I tip you off when I didn't know myself?"

I can think of only two Presidential press secretaries who could have handled the situation properly—Dwight D. Eisenhower's James Hagerty and Lyndon Johnson's George Reedy. Hagerty, who was in on every decision made by Eisenhower, was tough enough and respected enough to handle the nattering of the press. Reedy had a strong sense of responsibility. And working for a Democratic President, he would have been spared some of the recriminations of a liberal White House press corps.

Media's Demands

Neither Hagerty nor Reedy, moreover, would have had to contend with the current attitude of the press that no decision should be made by the President or the government which does not first have media concurrence. What was once known as the

"public's right to know" has since become the media's "right to determine." In effect, the press demands that it be part of the most sensitive decision-making process. It also claims the right to determine what is the national security. If it disagrees with the President or his advisers, you may be sure that disagreement will be aired on the news pages or TV evening news.

This is hardly an exaggeration. The Fourth Estate now acts as if it were the fourth arm of government—but first among its putative peers of executive, legislative and judicial. This is what "freedom of the press" has come to mean.

But it is not what the Founding Fathers had in mind when they wrote the First Amendment. "Congress shall make no law . . . abridging the freedom . . . of the press," the Constitution states. This does not mean that the press is categorically endowed with privileges and powers not accorded to the people—or that it can act independently of the laws and statutes of these United States. In fact, press insistence that by law it has rights of "confidentiality" not held by the citizenry is a violation of the spirit of the Bill of Rights.

The press now argues that in not divulging information which would have jeopardized the lives of 1,000 Americans, the government violated the First Amendment. The elasticity of this logic will win the huzzas of the American Civil Liberties Union and the entrenched left, but I doubt that it will impress the American people or the families of the Americans who were caught in the vortex of violence and criminality on the island of Grenada.

"Barring the press from reporting is dangerously wrong."

The Press Should Not Be Barred from Secret Military Maneuvers

David S. Broder

In the fall of 1983, a public furor arose when it became known that the US government had made the decision not to inform the press prior to the invasion of the island of Grenada. In the following viewpoint, David S. Broder, a liberal syndicated columnist, argues that in a free society, this kind of conduct is a dangerous form of censorship which could lead to government monopoly of information. It is vital, he says, that the American people recognize the danger of such "security" policies and act to prevent their recurrence.

As you read, consider the following questions:

1. Why, according to Mr. Broder, is the attitude wrong that the press should be banned if the government deems it prudent?
2. What does Mr. Broder mean by "monopoly of information"?
3. Why does Mr. Broder believe that it is the public's attitude, not that of the press or the government, which is really important?

David S. Broder, "The Grave Danger in Press Ban," *San Diego Tribune*, November 11, 1984. Reprinted with the author's permission.

My friend from Idaho, who is unshakably determined to convert one *Washington Post* columnist to the cause of true conservatism, called the other day. Had I noticed, she asked, that the first war the United States had won in almost 40 years was also the first where the blankety-blank reporters and photographers had been kept out of the way?

Leaving aside the question whether the takeover of Grenada from 600, 800, or 1,000 Cuban construction workers-soldiers and a melt-away local constabulary constitutes a war trophy, there is little doubt in my mind that the viewpoint implicit in her question has widespread support in this country.

At the Columbia University school of journalism, where the First Amendment has status almost equal to the First Commandment, a guest in the audience at a lecture last week was equally outspoken in her views. Not only was the Pentagon right to exclude journalists from covering the invasion, the military was more restrained than she would have been. Were it left to her, she said, any reporter or technician who showed up unwanted would have gotten the strafing that the commander of the Grenadian operation semi-facetiously (one hopes) threatened to unleash on any journalist he caught sneaking onto Grenada.

Crybabies of the Press

She was sick and tired, she added, of seeing reporters and cameramen harass the innocent victims of war. The scenes on television of the grieving families of the Marines killed in Beirut offended her, because they were intrusions into scenes of private grief, nor should the family members have been asked insensitive questions about their reactions to the devastating news.

In short, if the crybabies of the press feel unwanted, unappreciated and unloved because they were not invited ashore at Grenada, the heck with them. Who needs them anyway? If the president or the Pentagon think the press gets in the way of something important, then the president or the Pentagon has every right to keep them out.

That view is widespread, and it is flat-out wrong. We in the press need to acknowledge the failings and excesses that have earned us the enmity that is out there. But, whatever the tinge of special pleading in our brief, we have a clear obligation to say, once again, why prior restraint or barring the press from reporting is dangerously wrong.

Why Prior Restraint Is Wrong

It is wrong because control of information gives a government control over its citizens' minds. That is a power no government should have. It is a power the Constitution of the United States sought to deny our government permanently by the First Amendment.

Monopoly of information is the most dangerous monopoly of all. Cutting off electricity, or gas, or food or water is less dangerous to the citizens of a democracy than cutting off news. A government that cut off anything as tangible as food, water or power would immediately be challenged for the very act of denying those commodities. A government that cuts off information can keep the alarm bell from ringing—at least for a while.

Conservatives, of all people, should understand that those who want to keep government "off our backs" had better fight to keep government from taking over our brains. The real conservatives in the press corps understand this and have raised the alarm. No one has described the danger better than William Safire of *The New York Times,* who earlier in his career served as a speech writer and adviser to President Richard M. Nixon and Vice President Spiro Agnew.

As an expert on anti-press paranoia among politicians, Safire wrote last week, "The same vicious virus that infected the Nixon White House and caused its ruin is now raging through the Reagan administration . . . That contempt and hatred for an unelected elite led to the bunker mentality of 'Us against Them,' and then to an obsession with leaks and the excesses of Water-

IN THE NAME OF SAFETY

gate. The same baleful mood permeates the White House and the Pentagon today."

Safire writes as a conservative properly concerned that another conservative administration will destroy itself by succumbing to the temptation to control people's minds by controlling the news. His concern is justified, for relations between the White House and the press corps covering the Reagan administration have become as bitter the past 10 days as at any time since Nixon left office. One White House press aide has quit in protest of the administration's news-control policies, and an atmosphere of distrust exists which will not be easily dissipated.

But the larger question is not the character of the relationship between the press and the administration; both of those institutions are big enough to take care of themselves. The critical question is where the public comes down on the government's attempt to make itself the sole source of information about the military action in which American troops are planted on foreign soil with a declaration of war and with inevitable casualties and long-term military and diplomatic consequences.

The Will of the People

If the American people are willing to say that in such circumstances, it is acceptable to have reporters barred (or, in the case of those already on the scene, detained and denied the right to report what they had seen), then you may be assured the precedent will be followed.

The "blackout" will be extended the next time from 60 hours to six or 60 days. The principles of "safety" and "security" that were invoked to justify this case of censorship will be applied ever more broadly—and dangerously.

We in the press are not asking you to like us. Sometimes we do not like what we see each other doing. We are asking you to think—from your own self-interest—if you want to live in a society where the government is supreme.

"The argument that secrecy is essential to the nation's security . . . in reality reduces itself to an effort to keep the American people in the dark on matters that are of vital interest and concern to them."

The Press Should Have Access to Security Information

The People

In December 1984, a US space shuttle carrying secret cargo was launched. One national publication, *The Washington Post*, printed a story about the cargo despite a government request that no such information be published. The incident focused attention on the subject of government secrecy once again. In the following viewpoint, *The People*, a weekly socialist newspaper, argues that while there is some need for government secrecy, the growing trend is toward unnecessary censorship which steadily increases the power of the government and the military. Much of what the government tries to keep secret from the people is already known or easily discovered by the Soviet Union.

As you read, consider the following questions:

1. What does *The People* say is new about the current government secrecy policy?
2. How satisfied is *The People* with the media response to the government's tightened security?

"Military Shuttle Mission Highlights Growing Secrecy," *The People*, January 19, 1985. Reprinted by permission.

On Dec. 18, the public was informed that extraordinary measures would be invoked to assure secrecy regarding the military mission of the space shuttle launch scheduled for Jan. 23.

It was the first time in the history of the U.S. manned-space program that news coverage was to be severely curtailed. In fact, since 1958 and during all 46 of the U.S. space missions with crews, it has been the boast of NASA that the U.S. space program was an "open program" in sharp contrast to the Soviet Union's space program.

The implications of the new U.S. policy go far beyond the threat of keeping certain military matters cloaked in secrecy. In varying degrees and in various situations that practice has long been in vogue.

At least one earlier shuttle flight reportedly carried some secret military test equipment, the nature of which has never been disclosed by the Pentagon or NASA.

First Amendment Rights

The new policy, however, is a menacing step—both quantitatively and qualitatively—in the direction of curtailing the exercise of First Amendment rights.

It is not insignificant that the public announcement of the secrecy measures was made not by a civilian spokesperson for the Defense Department or the administration, but by a Pentagon spokesperson, Brig. Gen. Richard Abel of the U.S. Air Force. Nor was the warning, ostensibly aimed at the news media, limited to a prohibition of publication of specific information regarding the mission. The mere speculation on the possible nature of the shuttle's payload would be subject to investigation, Abel said.

The primary rationalization offered to justify the secrecy is that it is necessary, as Abel put it, to "deny our adversaries" any information which might reveal the identity of the mission or payloads.

When subsequently, *The Washington Post* published an article discussing the scheduled launch, Secretary of Defense Caspar W. Weinberger angrily reemphasized the Pentagon's rationalization. He charged that the *Post's* failure to be guided by the Pentagon's demand for silence was the "height of journalistic irresponsibility" and argued that the publication of such stories "can only give aid and comfort to the enemy."

Soviet Intelligence-Gathering

Aside from the fact that the United States is neither at war nor under military attack, hence not subject even to the questionable practice of wartime censorship, the secrecy argument is an utter sham. It is generally acknowledged that the Soviets have ample means to learn of the launch and to track the shuttle in flight

They're worried about terrorists? No, the Press.

FORT WHITE HOUSE

ROTHCO

© Whittemore/Rothco

without honing in on the U.S. media.

Soviet ships equipped with electronic devices and other surveillance equipment regularly monitor the activities both at Cape Canaveral on the East Coast and Vandenberg Air Force Base on the West Coast. And Soviet satellites are equipped not only to know within seconds when a U.S. space shot has been made but also to track them through space. As the president of the American Society of Newspaper Editors observed, "the ones who are really unaware of what is going on "are members of the American public."

In short, the argument that secrecy is essential to the nation's security from some foreign "adversary" or "enemy" in reality reduces itself to an effort to keep the American people in the dark on matters that are of vital interest and concern to them.

Floyd Abrams, an attorney who specializes in constitutional law summed it up succinctly when he stated, "It is plainly an effort to limit the scope and breadth of public debate on an important and controversial aspect of American public policy." He was referring, of course, to the militarization of space.

There are sound reasons to conclude that the Pentagon's imposition of secrecy on the Jan. 23 shuttle launch is another step in the Reagan administration's policy of increasingly restricting the flow of information to the American people particularly with regard to matters related to arms development and military activities.

Moreover, in the very nature of things, it would be naive not to realize that even greater restrictions will be imposed as the additional already planned military shuttle flights become fairly routine. As *The New York Times* reported, Air Force officials have "generally conceded" the point "that many of the news restrictions on the January flight were important more for the conditions [read, precedents] they would establish for future operations rather than for what they could or would hide on that particular flight."

In another article the *Times* noted: "Some journalists saw the new tightened security measures as part of a broad move by the government toward more secrecy. As examples, several cited efforts by the Reagan administration to amend the Freedom of Information Act to limit access and the Pentagon's policy to barring the press from the early stages of the invasion of Grenada."

One might have expected a spontaneous outburst of outrage from the media, the Congress and the public at the Pentagon's brazen threat. That was not the case. As was also the case with respect to the Grenada invasion, the media responses were characteristically lacking in principle.

People's Right to Know

The media generally agreed that there is a need for government secrecy. They were generally willing to play ball—to suppress information that the Pentagon might judge to be sensitive. They noted that historically they have always cooperated with the government on national security measures, etc. And though some made a point about the "right of the public" to information that might be relevant to an ongoing discussion of some particular policy, emphasis on the paramount consideration of not only the right but the need of the people to know what its government was doing or was about to do was at best incidental.

In short, the Pentagon's plan for peacetime censorship of the news, ostensibly for national security reasons, gives another boost to the military's growing influence on public policies. It will be at their peril if the workers of America fail to recognize the menace to what is left of our democratic rights in the growing tendency of the ruling class to cede decision and control of vital public policies to the military.

> "This act of willful perversity was a defiant
> statement . . . that [the press, not the
> administration], will determine which national
> security secrets shall remain classified."

The Press Should Not Be Trusted with Security Information

Patrick J. Buchanan

In December 1984, despite government requests to the contrary, *The Washington Post* published a story about the secret cargo of a US satellite. This created a furor among members of both the government and the media, bringing into question the extent to which the press can be trusted with information relating to national security. In the following viewpoint, Patrick J. Buchanan, a conservative syndicated columnist, deplores the indiscretion, and possible disloyalty, of the *Post*. It is this kind of episode, he says, that reinforces the idea that the press cannot be trusted.

As you read, consider the following questions:

1. For what reason, according to Mr. Buchanan, did *The Washington Post* publish information the government deemed secret?
2. Why does Mr. Buchanan believe that the First Amendment's guarantee of a free press does not apply in cases like the one cited in this viewpoint?

Patrick J. Buchanan, "Journalistic Responsibility'?", *The Washington Inquirer*, December 28, 1984. Reprinted by permission: Tribune Media Services.

Wednesday morning, the *Washington Post* gave a convincing demonstration why some Washington-based journalists cannot be trusted with military secrets—why the instinctive Pentagon decision to keep the press in the dark about Grenada was eminently correct.

On Page 1, the *Post* ran a story on the super-secret "sigint" satellite that the space shuttle *Discovery* is to carry into orbit in January. The story described the weight and configuration of the satellite, listed its purpose, and detailed the sort of information it hoped to pick up from Soviet missile tests. The story was produced by the same reporter who spear-headed the *Post's* campaign against the neutron weapon years ago, a campaign that dove-tailed nicely with the successful Soviet propaganda effort to prevent that anti-tank weapon's deployment in Western Europe.

Half a dozen news agencies had the same story as the *Post*. All of them, however, including the authoritative *Aviation Week & Space Technology*, honored personal requests from the secretary of defense not to publish; yet, the Post plunged ahead. Why?

Press Arrogance

In a word, arrogance. This act of willful perversity was a defiant statement by the *Post* to the United States Air Force, and to the Reagan administration, that we, not you, will determine which national security secrets shall remain classified. Defending its decision to publish, the *Post* conceded as much. When someone tells us a report we are about to publish threatens national security, the *Post* asserted, "*We* listen and *we* decide what to do." (emphasis added)

That reporters and editors at the *Post* are like the rest of us, U.S. citizens with identical obligations to protect our country's military secrets, is a concept utterly alien to the street elite.

Seeing details of the secret mission laid out in the morning paper, Defense Secretary Weinberger denounced the story as the "height of journalistic irresponsibility," and accused the *Post* of possibly having given "aid and comfort to the enemy," the very definition of treason. Good for Cap. Let's get it out front.

Post editor Benjamin Bradlee claimed that, "virtually every fact we mentioned is a matter of public record." But, if this was all recycled news, why did the Post display the story with such prominence on Page 1?

Comparative Security Violations

Ours is truly a remarkable society. An employee at TRW who turns over secrets to the Soviets on a previous intelligence satellite, Big Bird, is put in a federal penitentiary for life. An Air Force officer who violated the secretary's instructions and put out information on this satellite would be cashiered and court-martialed for a breach of faith. But the *Post*, blabbing it all on Page 1, is supposedly an advancer of democratic dialogue.

To continue regarding the *Washington Post* as simply a newspaper is like describing Rasputin as a simple parish priest. As an institution, the *Washington Post* is as partisan as the Democratic National Committee, and about as ideologically unbiased and neutral as the Institute for Policy Studies. Its staff contains numerous ideologues and partisans who simply double as "reporters." On issues like rebuilding America's strategic arsenal and recapturing Nicaragua from the communists, the *Washington Post*—institutionally as well as editorially—is on the opposite side from the government of the United States. The First Amendment rights it constantly invokes are used as levers to pry out information and expose secrets that will advance its own agenda and cripple the administration.

Hiding Behind the First Amendment

Counter-attacked, the *Post* routinely retreats behind the skirts of the First Amendment, reciting its patented J-school litany about "the people's right to know." But the American people were not clamoring to know the purposes, capabilities and launch details of this satellite the Air Force is sending up to advance the national security. The *Post* was simply salivating to expose the secret, to affront the national administration.

Reprinted with permission.

Unfortunately, the Reagan administration has declined to caution the American people to adopt the same attitude of suspicion and distrust toward the *Washington Post* and its ilk that the latter take toward the Reagan administration. The last election showed which of the two was "out of touch" with the American people.

This episode was not without its ironic aspect. Up on the screen Thursday night, CBS, taking the *Post's* side, threw up the stamp of "censorship." Which is a nice way of describing what the networks and major organizations did last fall with the gathering of evidence of mob connections to the family of the feminist they had helped to foist onto the ticket with the hapless Walter Mondale.

"The chief effect of the flood of libel judgments has not been to make [controversial exposés of wrongdoing] more accurate but to decrease their numbers."

Libel Suits Inhibit a Free Press

Martin Garbus

The question of how free the press should be to print uncomplimentary material about persons and organizations has long been debated. Many journalists believe that while they have a responsibility to be accurate and truthful in their reporting, they should be free to write whatever is true regardless of the effect. In the following viewpoint, Martin Garbus, a New York trial lawyer who often represents libel litigants, supports the press. He claims that nuisance suits and suits costing large amounts of time and money do not improve the press's ethics or accuracy. In fact, they make the press overly cautious and discourage its responsible exposure of wrongs.

As you read, consider the following questions:

1. Why, according to Mr. Garbus, are libel suits particularly hazardous to small publications and broadcast stations?
2. Mr. Garbus states that journalism which is most needed, that which exposes wrongdoing, is most vulnerable to litigation. Why does he think this is a bad thing?
3. What are some of his suggestions to reform libel law so that both the press and the public are protected?

The reality—and threat—of being sued for libel has left some of American journalism in a state of siege. Supreme Court rulings and the attitudes of libel juries have forced many newspapers to desperate efforts to avoid any error that could possibly be used as the basis for a lawsuit.

The drastic cutback in summary judgments, which used to eliminate many nuisance and harassment suits at an early stage, has brought down a blizzard of claims. The Church of Scientology, for example, has filed dozens of libel claims. One woman who has delivered speeches critical of Scientology has been sued for libel 17 times by the organization.

Most vulnerable are the nation's smaller publications and local television and radio stations. They play a vital role in exposing private and governmental incompetence and corruption, but they can easily be driven into bankruptcy if they are forced to defend even a single libel suit.

In 1979, for instance, *The Point Reyes Light,* a 3,100-circulation weekly newspaper in northern California, published a series of articles based on an investigation of Synanon, the drug rehabilitation center. The series brought the paper a Pulitzer Prize but led to four libel suits, seeking a total of more than $1 billion.

Destructive Fear of Libel

The fear of libel has also spread to major publications and the television networks. A major expansion has occurred in the number of libel-insurance policies and in the total premiums paid by the media.

Press spokesmen routinely deny that they kill articles because of the risk of libel, but the chilling effect is well known to lawyers who work with the media. In my own practice, I have found that publishers who once asked me whether the subject of an article could win a lawsuit, now ask simply, "Will he sue?" More and more, I see unflattering adjectives removed, incisive analyses of people and events watered down, risky projects dropped.

Similar experiences are reported by attorneys when libel issues are discussed. At a recent board meeting of the American Civil Liberties Union, for example, a number of case histories were offered. Typical was the publishing house that canceled the second printing of a book, and the paperback edition, after a libel complaint that was eventually shown to have no legal base.

When judges and jurors make an award of thousands of dollars against a newspaper in punitive damages, there is usually an assumption on their part that the award will deter the paper from printing falsehoods. And such judgments, or the threat of them, may indeed cause the media to go to even greater lengths to check their facts. That option may not, however, be feasible for financially hard-pressed publications or broadcasters, since it typically involves hiring larger staffs and paying high fees to have lawyers screen articles for potentially libelous statements.

Moreover, as a practical matter, the truth is hard to come by. It is nearly impossible for a publisher of thousands of books, a television news program that presents hundreds of facts daily or a newspaper that must meet daily deadlines to determine the ultimate truth of most of the controversial facts they deal with. And the operative word is "controversial."

Controversy Is Vulnerable

By definition, those aspects of journalism that are most in need of being defended under the First Amendment—the articles that expose wrongdoing or offer critical judgments on the powerful —are the most controversial and the most suceptible to litigation. The chief effect of the flood of libel judgments has not been to make such articles more accurate but to decrease their numbers. By that amount, free speech has been diminished.

The Death of Advocacy

In a recent survey on the effect of libel suits on newspapers, Gil Cranberg, professor of journalism at the University of Iowa, quotes the editor of a paper in a small Louisiana town: "I have to ask myself sometimes, Is this story worth $30,000 in attorneys' fees?" Cranberg also talked to a New Jersey editor who spends at least 10 percent of his editorial budget for lawyers: "If these suits keep up, advocacy journalism of any kind will be dead."

Nat Hentoff, *The Progressive*, May 1983.

The Burger Court's decision in the suit brought by Col. Anthony Herbert, giving his attorneys access to the materials used by "60 Minutes" in the preparation of the TV segment, has greatly added to the media's nervousness and confusion. Some media lawyers, for example, suggest that reporters and editors throw out their interview notes, first drafts and any communications dealing with controversial stories. Other lawyers suggest that all interviews should be taped and the tape carefully saved.

Investigative journalism has decreased in recent years in large part because of the threat of libel awards. And the atmosphere created by the awards has also changed the focus of investigation by many journalists. Since, under current law, it is so much safer to print controversial material about public officials than about private citizens, publishers are rapidly becoming disenchanted with hard-hitting books and articles about private citizens.

Threat from Wealthy

Much of the threat, however, comes from a certain class of private citizen: the wealthy ones. Most private persons hire libel attorneys on a contingency basis; that is, the attorney is willing to invest his time without fee on the chance of victory and a one-third share in the money award or settlement. But one often-overlooked result of the libel-law revolution has been that networks and major publishers have hired sophisticated attorneys who know how to run up litigation costs on a plaintiff and drive him from the courthouse. Only such citizens as the owners of the Rancho LaCosta resort, currently suing *Penthouse* magazine—they claim they were wrongly identified as connected with organized crime—can afford to pay the legal fees lawyers usually demand to take on the likes of Penthouse....

Twenty years ago, when the Supreme Court decided *New York Times v. Sullivan,* it was clear that the libel law as it then existed was not working. Because of the uproar over civil rights and the response of the Southern states, juries were using the law to hold the press hostage. Today, though the nation has changed in so many ways, there is a certain similarity in the conditions confronting the press. Once again, we see huge awards levied against the media by juries who often see the press as an enemy of the people; once again, we see the Supreme Court preparing to confront the issues.

Proposed Remedies

The legal fraternity has not been shy about its own ideas. One proposal, for example, seeks a law that would make an appropriate correction in an offending newspaper acceptable as a substitute for a lawsuit. Other suggestions focus on the role of the jury. One would eliminate punitive awards on the basis that the Founding Fathers never envisioned that a jury would be deciding appropriate behavior for an institution protected under the First Amendment. Another would eliminate compensatory awards for "mental anguish" on the basis that objective evidence is seldom available.

The most significant reform offered, though, addresses a question that has been pondered by generations of judges: Is not the law of libel as it affects public affairs inherently incompatible with the First Amendment guarantees of freedom of speech? Justice Hugo L. Black, in his opinion on the Sullivan case, put it this way: "I doubt that a country can live in freedom where its people can be made to suffer physically or financially for criticizing their government, its actions or its officials."

Those doubts, however, do not appear to be uppermost in the minds of the majority of today's Supreme Court. Nor do American juries show much concern about the effects their rulings have had on the press. As a result, one of America's basic freedoms is at risk.

> "Putting the spotlight on high beam tends to keep folks on the straight and narrow."

Libel Suits Improve the Integrity of the Press

Ben Wattenberg

A recent libel suit, *Ariel Sharon vs. Time Magazine,* focused public attention on questions of journalistic ethics and reliability. The jury, after several months and millions of dollars of legal costs, decided that *Time* inaccurately reported that Israel's defense minister encouraged the massacre of Palestinian refugees but that the report was published as a result of human error and not with malicious intent. In the following viewpoint, Ben Wattenberg, a nationally syndicated columnist and a fellow at the American Enterprise Institute, argues that despite the costs of such trials, they do make the media reassess their own methods and become more responsible.

As you read, consider the following questions:

1. According to Mr. Wattenberg, journalists claim that such things as libel suits are harmful to the media. Why?
2. Why does Mr. Wattenberg disagree with this idea?
3. What kind of pressure does Mr. Wattenberg say is most effective in improving the media?

Ben Wattenberg, "Making the Press Better," *The Washington Times,* January 30, 1985. © 1985 United Feature Syndicate.

There was something heartening about the reaction to the conclusion of the *Ariel Sharon vs. Time* magazine case.

Consider: Normally—with but one exception—the view of the journalistic community is that the press does good work by putting the pressure on the major institutions in a democracy. Talk to your mainstream media man and you'll find out he believes that, when the press puts the heat on government, then government cleans up its act. When the press puts the spotlight on business, media man says that will make business behave more responsibly.

There can be excesses in this view—I have, in fact, written about those excesses—but it is essentially true: Putting the spotlight on high beam tends to keep folks on the straight and narrow.

Pressure "Chills" Journalism

The one exception to this rule, to hear journalists tell it as they have heretofore told it, is the press itself. Pressure, we have been told, is not good for journalism. You see, it has a "chilling effect." If people criticize these tender flowers in medialand, we have been told, they will be afraid to stand up brave and strong and clean and true. (Just imagine a wilted Sam Donaldson.) If—heaven forfend—a politician criticizes the press, he is described as "Agnewesque," and the fear is that government will start pulling television licenses. If businessmen punch back, the fear is that they will hold back advertising.

But this time it was different. The press joined in the press-bashing. Almost every journalistic competitor called *Time* "arrogant." It's a pretty good word. *Time* was wrong; they seriously defamed a man; they have refused to acknowledge any real error.

The *Time* folks are all harrumphing about how they do not intend to change any of their practices. Don't believe that. The people at *Time* may be arrogant, but they are not stupid. They've spent millions of dollars on lawyers, have been found guilty of two major charges by a serious jury, have seen their reputation damaged, have faced the scorn of their colleagues.

You'd better believe that they will review their procedures, and think twice before they again cavalierly imply that someone encouraged the slaying of women and children.

Pressure Works

Pressure works. It works on government, just as the press says. It works on business, just as the press says. And it works on the press, too, as the press has not liked to say. It makes them better.

Of course, the threat of a libel suit can cure only a very small part of what's wrong with the American press. Most items on television or in the newspaper do not touch on libel or defamation. Stories about politics, the economy, business, and science may, on any given occasion, be wrongheaded, mis-emphasized, exaggerated, inaccurate, and misleading—but they are not libelous.

But there are other forms of pressure that make journalists better, too. When conservatives began screaming that the media were too liberal, the reaction from the media moguls was about what *Time's* was to the Sharon verdict. Not us! How dare you! Chilling effect! But then they went back to their boardrooms and asked: Is there some truth to the charge?

There was. I sense the media are somewhat more balanced these days. Pressure works.

Pressure Needed

During the Lebanon war, the Jewish community in America jumped up and down about the perceived anti-Israel bias in the television coverage. The networks denied it, but took a second look. Coverage seems fairer now. Pressure works.

No "Chilling Effect"

There are no signs that the big news media have been scared off tough but important stories when they have the proof needed to publish or broadcast. More careful, yes—but what's wrong with that so long as constitutional protections remain intact?

Richard M. Clurman, *The Washington Post National Weekly Edition,* March 11, 1985.

Public opinion polls have shown that many viewers are fed up with a steady drumbeat of sensationalized bad news. The networks have tried to respond.

The most constructive form of pressure on journalism—and the safest form—can and should come from other journalists. They can't be accused of chilling the press.

The press has become very wealthy and extremely influential in recent years. They must be treated as big boys and girls now, subject to the same intense scrutiny by the media that other big-time players get.

"The fairness doctrine in particular has guaranteed balance and diversity on the air."

Broadcasting Should Be Subject to Content Regulation

Pat Aufderheide

Traditionally the broadcast media (radio and television) have been subject to government regulation. Initially regulations were established to prevent undue influence on the public by the limited number of broadcasting organizations. In the following viewpoint, Pat Aufderheide, a Washington-based writer and contributing editor of *In These Times,* explains why regulation is still necessary even though the number of possible broadcast channels has become almost infinite.

As you read, consider the following questions:

1. Ms. Aufderheide quotes the Reverend Everett Parker as saying that "Freedom of expression is cut into by conglomerate holdings." What does Reverend Parker mean?
2. According to Ms. Aufderheide, why do public interest advocates argue that continuing regulation is necessary?

Pat Aufderheide, "Free Speech for Broadcasters Only," *The Nation*, September 1, 1984. *The Nation* magazine, Nation Associates, Inc. © 1984.

Senator Robert Packwood, powerful chairman of the Commerce Committee which oversees communications issues, has found a cause worth building a bandwagon for: what he calls "First Amendment rights for broadcasters." On the face of it, nothing sounds more patriotic or less controversial than extending First Amendment rights. Packwood's plan to free broadcasters from government regulation, however, radically challenges current policy—and some say it could undermine freedom of speech.

The 1934 Communications Act asserts that radio and television stations must act in the public interest in return for their monopoly licenses to use the airwaves, a limited resource which belongs to the American people. By applying the fairness doctrine and by requiring license renewal hearings every seven years, the government has sought to regulate the industry.

Packwood believes modern technology and business organizations have made such oversight unnecessary. Because, thanks to cable and satellite technology, television sets can pick up a large number of channels, and because telephones and computers can receive electronic messages, he argues, the marketplace will foster diversity of viewpoints by itself. Furthermore, since a TV station, a newspaper and a data service might all be owned by the same conglomerate, it is discriminatory to single out broadcasters for regulation.

Corporate Logic

Media corporations love that logic, and so do telecommunications companies like A.T.&T. and I.B.M. Advertisers love it too. Under the present system, broadcasters say they are sometimes leery of advocacy or issue advertising because they fear that owing to the fairness doctrine they will have to provide equal time for those holding opposing views. The most eager supporters of broadcasters' liberation, though, are media conglomerates, which are increasingly acquiring holdings in both the broadcast and print industries. Since 1949, the number of newspaper-owned television stations has more than doubled, and a recent industry poll of a thousand newspapers showed that two-thirds were either involved in television or were about to be.

Not everyone thinks diversity in the marketplace of ideas is exemplified by a range that spans *People, Money* and Home Box Office, all owned by Time Inc. The Rev. Everett Parker, former head of the United Church of Christ's Office of Communications and considered the founder of the public interest media movement, thinks the airwaves are still a scarce resource. "If you want to test it, try to start a radio station in New York," he says. Besides, scarcity or no scarcity, the airwaves belong to the public. But here's the clincher: "Freedom of expression is cut into by conglomerate holdings," he says. "If there is competition, it is between effective monopolies for rating points. Government licensees are asking to set themselves up to do what government cannot, which is to determine what voices shall be heard."

Scarcity Requires Regulation

We have yet to see the tremendous new diversity in video sources with which Chairman Fowler justifies the repeal of the Fairness Doctrine. Today, only one in four U.S. households receives cable services; less than one percent of these homes had subscription television (STV) at the end of 1980; and less than one-half of one percent received the Multipoint Distribution Service (MDS, a microwave system). Projections are that in 1990 roughly fifty percent of the U.S. households will still be without cable services. . . .

What these factors suggest is that even if optimistic projections on the growth of cable, MDS, STV, and DBS (Direct Broadcast Satellite) eventually became reality, we will continue to operate in a climate of scarcity for some time to come. Hence, we will continue to need the protection afforded by the fairness provision against abuse caused by that scarcity.

John D. Dingell, in *Mass Media Issues*, edited by George Rodman, 1984.

Whose First Amendment is it, anyway—the corporations' or the people's? The famous Supreme Court case *Red Lion v. Federal Communications Commission* in 1969 put it boldly: "The right of the viewers and listeners, not the right of the broadcasters" comes first. Corporate free speech will come at the expense of individuals, argues Andrew Schwartzman of the Media Access Project, a public interest law firm in Washington specializing in media issues. At the San Francisco-based Public Media Center, a public interest advertising agency, Herbert Chao Gunther voices a similar view: "If corporations want the free speech rights of individuals, then they ought to be liable to capital punishment too."

Inhibition of Freedom?

Broadcasters argue that regulation inhibits freedom of speech: to avoid the risk of having to provide free or cheap air time to opposing views and to all political candidates, they eschew controversy. But public interest advocates argue that the fairness doctrine in particular has guaranteed balance and diversity on the air, frequently in ways invisible to the Federal Communications Commission because complaints are settled privately in meetings between citizen groups and station owners. The fairness doctrine is perhaps most commonly invoked by citizens during local referendums in order to counter expensive, blanket ad campaigns by powerful interests. Recently the nuclear energy industry and the beverage container industry (bucking returnable-bottle laws) have been the targets of such citizen action.

"First Amendment rights for broadcasters" is thus a radical departure from tradition. Senator Packwood knows that, and he is prepared for a long fight. . . .

He introduced the Freedom of Expression Act, which would abolish the fairness doctrine, its equal-time provisions and the F.C.C.'s watchdog function, monitoring broadcasters' fulfillment of their public interest obligations. . . .

In the House, Packwood's proposals have been greeted with hostility and intransigence by key players on communications issues. Representative John Dingell, who chairs the Energy and Commerce Committee, has promised to block Packwood's project, saying, "Fairness and equal time are not matters which are subject to negotiation." . . .

Government Support

But he'll get plenty of support from President Reagan's appointees in the government.

The F.C.C. under Mark Fowler, who believes the commission should become a "traffic cop," confining itself to assigning frequencies, has worked hard over the last three years to deregulate broadcasting. It has already lifted most regulations from commercial television, and in the spring it issued an inquiry into the fairness doctrine. The inquiry boldly asked why it should not be abolished. (Traditionally F.C.C. inquiries are at least phrased more objectively.) The first round of comments will be filed on September 6, and the second round is due November 8. But commissioner Mimi Dawson would like instead to launch an omnibus inquiry asking why the F.C.C. should be involved in content regulation at all. Meanwhile, the Supreme Court has hinted that it might reconsider the constitutionality of content regulation, depending on the results of the F.C.C. inquiry.

Americans could pay a high price if Packwood's idea wins popular support, warn public interest advocates. Says Herbert Chao Gunther: "The hoopla about 1984 is getting passé, but the reality is being flaunted in front of us, and Packwood is right out there. If anything can turn this country in a homogenous, undemocratic and dangerous direction, it is the kind of ill-thought-through concept that Packwood is endorsing."

"[Broadcast regulations] violate the fundamental premise of the First Amendment —our government has no business determining who is permitted to say what."

Broadcasting Should Not Be Subject to Content Regulation

Bob Packwood

Since 1934, electronic media—radio and, later, television—have been subject to a number of regulations about what can be broadcast. The Fairness Doctrine is one example: While newspapers and magazines do not have to present both sides of an issue, the electronic media must. If they broadcast a report or a speech on a controversial or political issue, they must offer an equal amount of time to proponents of other sides of the same issue. In the following viewpoint, Senator Bob Packwood (Republican, Oregon), chairman of the Senate Commerce Committee, argues that today to present a wide variety of views there is an unlimited number of broadcast channels available. Consequently, the electronic media should be subject to no more content regulation than the print media.

As you read, consider the following questions:

1. List the five types of broadcast regulation Senator Packwood describes.
2. Why does Senator Packwood believe that such regulation is unfair and unnecessary?

Bob Packwood, "Full Freedom of Expression for the Media," reprinted from *USA Today*, March 1984. Copyright 1984 by the Society for the Advancement of Education.

When the publisher and editors of *USA Today* decided to print this article, the decision was theirs alone. They do not have to worry about how the government reacts to their editorial judgments. No Federal agency can review the contents of their magazine and order that material be added or deleted, much less order that the magazine be shut down entirely. The First Amendment protects *USA Today* from those kinds of infringements. It says, "Congress shall make no law . . . abridging the freedom of speech, or of the press. . . ." It is concise and emphatic, and it forms the foundation upon which all of our other freedoms are built.

If, however, I were speaking these words to you over radio or television, we would face an entirely different situation. The station's management, in deciding whether to broadcast these words, would be deeply concerned about possible government reactions. Broadcasters *are* regulated by a Federal agency which reviews their programming decisions. It can bring them before its commissioners or before a court of law to justify their actions. It can shut a station down altogether by revoking its government license. For the electronic media, the First Amendment might well read, "Congress shall make no law . . . abridging the freedom of speech, or of the press (except in matters involving the electronic media)."

Content Regulations

Thus, our nation's media are divided into a two-class society. The print media are fully protected, but the electronic media are subjected to content regulations. Here are just a few examples:
• Broadcasters are licensed for limited terms and may have these licenses suspended, revoked, or not renewed if they do not operate in the government-defined "public interest."
• Stations must devote a substantial amount of time to the discussion of "public issues."
• A station which presents one side of an issue must provide opportunity for the presentation of contrasting views on that issue.
• The FCC limits the ability of broadcasters to editorialize.
• Broadcasters' licenses can be revoked if they deny airtime to Federal candidates; once a candidate obtains airtime, other candidates for the same office must receive equal time.
• Rates for political airtime are regulated.

None of these regulations could be applied to the print media, and all of them violate the fundamental premise of the First Amendment—our government has no business determining *who* is permitted to say *what.* I believe that premise holds true whether a message is shouted from a soapbox, printed on a pamphlet, broadcast over a radio, or beamed from a satellite. I believe further that we must act to ensure that electronic speech receives the protection which it deserves. . . .

The subordinate First Amendment status of broadcasters should be troubling to the print media. Communications technology is moving in directions which are making even the most complacent in the press wake up to the impending danger. The print media and the electronic media are converging in ways which may soon undercut pleas for the First Amendment protection for publishers.

What will *USA Today,* for example, look like 10 or 20 years from now? In the not so distant future, *USA Today* and other printed material could be available in several different formats, each based on *electronic* distribution.

A printed version of *USA Today* probably will always be available, but it may be edited in a central location, with the page layouts beamed by satellite to regional printing presses. (The *Wall Street Journal* and other papers use this technology today.) You also may be printing your own copy of *USA Today* in your home. The magazine could be transmitted via telephone or cable lines, or by terrestrial or satellite signals to your home terminal's printer. For some readers, *USA Today* may never be on paper at all. You may choose to browse among totally electronic "pages" which are "printed" on your video screen.

How will the government handle that kind of "press?" Will the First Amendment protect *USA Today* of the future from content regulations? Or will it, like the broadcasters, be subject to government regulations merely because it utilizes electronic methods of distribution?

Timely Issues

Technological forces are making freedom of expression issues especially timely and these same forces are making old fears about scarcity obsolete. We must not continue down the path on which tradition, complacency, unthinking application of precedent, and outright error have led the U.S.

We are living in an era of rapid and explosive communications development. Scarcity may have been a reasonable concern during the 1920's and 1930's, but today's problem is keeping track of communications abundance.

Radio broadcasting, of course, has grown far beyond the confines of its infancy, and newer methods of communication seem to be appearing at an ever-increasing rate. Our nation now has over 9,000 radio stations and over 1,000 television stations. Cable systems using coaxial cable can provide hundreds of channels; future systems utilizing optical fibers could provide even more. Low-power broadcasting, microwave channels, and direct satellite-to-home broadcasting will further expand communications options.

Communications technology is advancing at such a rapid rate that even experts cannot predict what the future will bring. They stress, however, that scarcity is no longer an issue. Any limitations on our communications abundance will be caused by economic constraints or by government regulation itself, not by technological shortcomings. Spectrum scarcity simply cannot be used to justify government controls which fly in the face of our First Amendment rights.

The diversity of electronic voices which the government's content regulations were intended to provide (but never did) can be achieved by opening up all of these new methods of communication to freedom. If these technologies are allowed to be free, they can be as diverse as the world of print—all to the benefit of the public. Some electronic outlets, like some papers and magazines, will appeal to a wide, national audience. Others will aim for local or specialized markets. All of them will be able to seek their fair share of the interested public, if they are freed from stifling governmental obligations.

Ensuring Full Protection

How can we best ensure that the electronic media gain full protection? Our nation's founders surely would have guaranteed full protection if they could have foreseen these technological advances. . . .

I believe that the only effective and permanent solution is a constitutional solution. I have proposed that we add an amendment to our Constitution which would guarantee that electronic communications are protected from government regulation after we have exhausted statutory relief. While this could be a long and arduous process, the goal is certainly worthwhile. We have no other means of guaranteeing a permanent right—freedom of expression—which is as important. I believe it is a cause worth fighting for, a cause which would guarantee freedom of expression well into the future.

Evaluating Sources of Information

A critical thinker must always question sources of information. Historians, for example, usually distinguish between *primary sources (eyewitness accounts)* and *secondary sources (writings or statements based on primary or eyewitness accounts or on other secondary sources)*. A diary kept by a spy is an example of a primary account. An article by a journalist based on that diary is a secondary source.

In order to read and think critically, one must be able to recognize primary sources. However, this is not enough. Eyewitness accounts do not always provide accurate descriptions. Historians may find ten different eyewitness accounts of an event and all the accounts might interpret the event differently. The historians must then decide which of these accounts provide the most objective and accurate interpretations.

Test your skill in evaluating sources of information by completing the following exercise. Pretend that your teacher tells you to write a research report about whether or not the press endangers US security. You decide to include an equal number of primary and secondary sources. Listed below are a number of sources which may be useful in your research. Carefully evaluate each of them. Then, *place a P next to those descriptions you believe are primary sources.* Second, *rank the primary sources* assigning the number (1) to what appears to be the most objective and accurate primary source, the number (2) to the next most objective, and so on until the ranking is finished. *Repeat the entire procedure, this time placing an S next to those descriptions you feel would serve as secondary sources and then ranking them.*

If you are doing this activity as a member of a class or group, discuss and compare your evaluation with other members of the group. If you are reading this book alone, you may want to ask others if they agree with your evaluation. You will probably discover that others will come to different conclusions than you. Listening to their reasons may give you valuable insights in evaluating sources of information.

P = primary
S = secondary

1. *The Pentagon Papers*—a collection of government reports about US activities in Vietnam; these were "leaked" to the *New York Times* even though they were marked "Secret"
2. a newspaper editorial called "The Government Should Be Open to the Press"
3. a newspaper editorial called "Can the Press Be Trusted with Government Secrets? No Way!"
4. a novel about an investigative reporter who uncovers government corruption
5. A Pulitzer Prize-winning report about the methods the government uses to safeguard its secrets
6. an essay written by a Supreme Court Justice presenting her views on government secrecy and the press
7. a taped discussion, printed in a national magazine, between a top reporter and a top government official about the relationship between the press and the government
8. an essay by an avid defender of the First Amendment explaining why there should be no government policies that are secret from the public
9. a book called *A Free Press: A History from Colonial Days to the Present*
10. a printed interview with a refugee from Grenada telling how the actions of sensation-seeking US reporters inspired the violence in his country
11. an autobiography by a former *Washington Post* reporter in which he tells about the numerous stories he knew about but didn't print because of potential danger to the US
12. the editorial cartoon from viewpoint 4 of this chapter
13. viewpoint 3 from this chapter
14. an article by a top-notch conservative journalist discussing his belief that the government should trust the press's sense of responsibility about sensitive information
15. an article called "The Ten Most-Censored Government Stories"
16. an article by a top-notch reporter confessing that he knowingly printed top-secret information in one of his stories because "it was news"

Periodical Bibliography

The following list of periodical articles deals with the subject matter of this chapter.

Floyd Abrams	"Will the First Amendment Survive the 1980's?" *Vital Speeches of the Day*, April 15, 1985.
Jonathan Alter	"The Pentagon Tests the Press," *Newsweek*, May 6, 1985.
John V.R. Bull	"Punitive Damages," *Vital Speeches of the Day*, October 15, 1984.
John V.R. Bull	"Libel and the Media," *Vital Speeches of the Day*, March 15, 1985.
John R. Burke	"The One Un-American Act," *Vital Speeches of the Day*, February 1, 1984.
The Center Magazine	Special section on "Privacy, Government, and the Media," September/October 1982, November/December 1982. Available from the Center for Study Democratic Institution, Box 4068, Santa Barbara, CA 93108.
The Center Magazine	Forums on "The Grenada Experience: What Should Be the Role of the Media During Periods of Conflict?" and "The Media and Government Leaks," September/October 1984.
Harold Evans	"The Sharon Verdict," *U.S. News & World Report*, February 4, 1985.
Mark Fowler	"Unfair Is More to the Point," *Washington Times*, April 15, 1985.
Martin Garbus	"Abolish Libel—the Only Answer," *The Nation*, October 8, 1983.
Martin Garbus	"Wrong Case, Wrong Place, Wrong Result," *The Nation*, February 16, 1985.
Henry Grunwald	"Trying to Censor Reality," *Time*, November 7, 1983.
Richard Halloran	"Pentagon to Seek Increased Secrecy," *The New York Times*, December 21, 1984.
Harper's	Forum on "Can the Press Tell the Truth?" January 1985.
Jesse Helms	"The American People Deserve a Free Press," *Human Events*, March 30, 1985.

William A. Henry III	"Libel Law: Good Intentions Gone Awry," *Time*, March 4, 1985.
Reed Irvine	"'You Can Trust Us,' They Said," *Washington Inquirer*, December 28, 1984.
C. M. Kittrell	"There's No Such Thing as a Free Press," *Vital Speeches of the Day*, October 15, 1984.
Melvin F. Lasky	"Suspicion by Omission," *Encounter*, December 1984.
Gary McGrath	"Freedom of the Press," *The Freeman*, October 1984.
Drew Middleton	"Barring Reporters from the Battlefield," *The New York Times Magazine*, February 5, 1984.
Milton Mueller	"Let's Abolish the Federal Censorship Commission," *Inquiry*, February 1983.
Aryeh Neier	"The Case for a Right of Reply," *The Nation*, October 8, 1983.
The New Republic	"First Amendment Junkies," August 6, 1984.
Michael Parenti	"Does the U.S. Have a Free Press?" *The Witness*, March 1985.
The People	"Media Help Test Censorship Plans," May 25, 1985.
Carol E. Rinzler	"Who Is That Public Figure—And Why Can You Say All Those Terrible Things About Him?" *Publisher's Weekly*, June 24, 1983.
Walter Schneir and Miriam Schneir	"The Right's Attack on the Press," *The Nation*, March 30, 1985.
J. Carter Swain	"Censorship in a Free Society," *The Churchman*, March 1985.
J.E. Swearingen	"Responsibility in Journalism," *Vital Speeches of the Day*, March 15, 1985.
U.S. News & World Report	"Censor Journalists Covering War?" Pro and Con interviews with Vice Admiral William Mack (retired) and Jerry Friedheim, November 14, 1983.
Greg Warner	"Who Decides What Is on the Tube?" *Christianity Today*, April 8, 1983.

3 CHAPTER

Does National Security Justify Censorship?

Chapter Preface

For the protection of national security, the circulation of scientific, technical, military, and other information is often restricted. Scientists and academics often resent restrictions on the exchange of technical information because, they believe, such exchange furthers the cause of science and of the nation. Government officials, on the other hand, believe that unrestricted access to information makes the country vulnerable to unfriendly nations who can obtain such information and use it to counteract or to surpass US technology.

Information specifically related to government and/or military matters is another touchy area. In 1977 Frank Snepp, a former Central Intelligence Agency (CIA) operative, published a book based on his experiences in Vietnam while a CIA agent. The CIA reacted strongly, saying that Snepp had violated a lifetime agreement signed by all CIA personnel agreeing not to publish *anything*, both while a CIA employee *and* for the rest of his or her life, without receiving prior approval from the Agency. In 1980 in *Snepp v. United States*, the Supreme Court sided with the CIA, reinforcing the validity of lifetime security agreements.

In 1983, plagued by his perception of threats to the nation, President Ronald Reagan signed National Security Directive 84 which went much further than previous directives. Not limited to employees of security-sensitive agencies, Directive 84 required a broad range of government employees to sign lifetime security agreements similar to that of the CIA.

The viewpoints in this chapter debate the question of openness vs. secrecy in government.

"Many of the systems and many of the data bases . . . on the free market in our open society are the very ones that the Soviet Union will do anything to get."

Technical Information Must Be Restricted

Cecile Shure

Government officials, academicians, and scientists frequently argue about the conflict between national security and the sharing of information common among scholars and scientists. Most agree that there is a need for guarding some information carefully—but what and how much? Cecile Shure, the author of the following viewpoint, is a consultant with B-K Dynamics. She formerly served as a Special Assistant in the Office of the Deputy Secretary of Defense for International Economic, Trade, and Security Policy. As a frequent speaker on defense issues, she is strongly concerned about the potentially damaging information hostile nations can acquire merely by reading publicly circulated journals and by attending open scientific conferences.

As you read, consider the following questions:

1. List two examples of evidence Ms. Shure cites to prove that the Soviets have used openly available information about American technology to the detriment of the U.S.
2. Do you think Ms. Shure would like to see all exchange of scientific and technical information stopped? Explain your answer and decide whether you agree with her.

Reprinted by permission of the American Library Association, "Remarks," by Cecile Shure from *Newsletter on Intellectual Freedom*, September 1984.

I appreciate the opportunity to be here with you today. . . . Today, prior to this session, I was in the exhibit hall. . . . I was looking at some of the computer services that are being made available to libraries. It was very exciting—for awhile—to think of these wonderful opportunities in a free society. You have access to computers and high technology to teach, to grow, to learn, to provide information, and this is what it's all about. But I was brought back to reality very quickly because many of the systems and many of the data bases that I saw on the free market in our open society are the very ones that the Soviet Union will do anything to get. And unlike the Americans, the Soviets don't have to go before the Congress for budget processes; their priority is defense. They may not be able to do everything, but they can do anything and what they want they get, with the first priority being for defense. We use a CAT Scan for heart patients, they use it for defense.

Soviet Technology Theft

Two experiences that I've had come to mind (I'm going to be weaving in many of the things I've seen in the last few years while working on the whole question of international technology transfer.) The first thing that came to my mind was the IBM computers. Now, the Soviets have developed their own large computer that is comparable to the IBM 360. As a matter of fact, we know they got it from Western technology—they were attending a fair and were caught taking pictures. The interesting thing is that the Soviet software begins with a welcome to the IBM 360! So clearly they are taking our software and putting it to use.

A more recent example is something you probably read about in the newspapers in late December. In both Hamburg, Germany, and Stockholm, Sweden, ships were stopped on their way to the Soviet Union with components for a VAX computer, one of the most sophisticated computers in the world. Had the Soviets gotten that computer, they would have gained the technology to run anti-ballistic missile systems. Now, they are fantastic at reverse engineering. And what they would have done was run that computer system, learned how it worked while they developed an anti-ballistic missiles fire fighting system. So, there is a very basic dichotomy—we want to share with and grow and provide education, but we also have to live with the reality that the Soviet Union wants our technology and wants it for other than peaceful and educational purposes.

I want to present a hypothetical, but true, scenario. It addresses our situation.

Student Exchanges Dangerous

We've had a student exchange program with the Soviet Union. The Soviet student comes to America on a scientific exchange.

He's 38 years old, he's a Ph.D. nuclear physicist. He comes to America and goes to one of our universities. He can travel unrestricted. He can speak to anyone. He can have access to our American libraries, and subsequently, to our journals, publications, software, and data bases. He studies alongside our American scientist who is on the brink of discovering advanced technology which can in the future have defense implications.

The American student going to Russia, on the other hand, is age 24, and is working on his master's degree, in history or art. He cannot travel outside his host city; he cannot read or study anything beyond the designated discipline for which he came to Russia. He has no access to scientific data and he is not allowed into scientific labs.

KGB Sucking Up Information

Operating out of embassies, consulates, and so-called 'business delegations,' KGB operatives have blanketed the developed capitalist countries with a network that operates like a gigantic vacuum cleaner, sucking up formulas, patents, blueprints and know-how with frightening precision. We believe these operations rank higher in priority even than the collection of military intelligence . . . This network seeks to exploit the "soft underbelly"—the individuals who, out of idealism or greed, fall victim to intelligence schemes; our traditions of an open press and unrestricted access to knowledge; and finally, the desire of academia to jealously preserve its prerogatives as a community of scholars unencumbered by government regulation. Certainly, these freedoms provide the underpinning of the American way of life. It is time, however, to ask what price we must pay if we are unable to protect our secrets?

Lawrence J. Grady, quoted in *Physics Today,* February 1983.

Once home, the Soviet returns to his highly-valued government-sponsored job. And he brings his newly gained knowledge to the Soviet government labs where it is used to meet the needs of the Soviet government—again, defense is the primary goal. The American returns, goes back to his university and continues to work on his dissertation. The U.S. government does not have any requirements.

Touring Spies

A true case in point: A group of Soviet visitors asked to visit the Lockheed factory—they wanted to see the L1011, a commercial airliner. Shortly thereafter, the Soviet Union made a breakthrough in a long-desired capability with transports for military use. The breakthrough was a result of knowledge gained during their visit. How? Each one of those Soviet visitors was wearing sticky shoes, and as they walked through the plant, they were able to pick up the metals on their shoes—the very metals that gave them the breakthrough to gain the technology. . . .

A conference two years ago this summer basically kicked off a lot of what is going on today. It was a conference for the Society of Photo Optical Instrumental Engineers, more commonly known as the SPIES conference. Two days prior to the conference, 120 papers were pulled by the Defense Department, the reason being that this conference was both an international conference and a classified conference back-to-back. There were several Soviets attending and it was believed after a review of the titles of the papers to be presented that these 120 papers had data which could provide information to the Soviet Union. Now, interestingly enough, there were existing DOD regulations about prepublication review and about attendance at conferences by contractors. But in each and every case, including papers written by government workers, the papers had never been submitted to the government for any kind of review.

After the conference, when things simmered down—and after a lot of bad publicity for the Defense Department—the papers were reviewed. It turned out that there were very few that would have been pulled. But unfortunately in this circumstance, there was a lot of rash reaction from people who had not followed the regulations. . . .

Conference Dangers

Why are we so afraid of conferences if we feel we are not giving the scientists or the Soviet Union classified material? I think many people fear that the Soviets will come into these conferences and informally gather information on a one-to-one basis, picking up bits and pieces. It's very, very clear that they spend a lot of time checking out conferences, reading and seeing what's being given in public places. Let me give an example. The American Defense Preparedness Association Plastics and Chemical Job Symposium was advertised in our local journals and in local magazines. It was held at the Four Seasons Hotel in the Lake of the Ozarks in October, 1983. The Old Crows Electronic Warfare Technical Symposium was held at Virginia Beach. Now, everyone knows that *Aviation Week* is widely read in the Soviet Union. It goes on Washington newsstands on Monday and they say the first two copies are on the first airplane going to the Soviet Union. By the time it gets there, it's translated into Russian. And every time you open up *Aviation Week,* there's a list of every one of these technical conferences. So even if they're not attending because it's classified, they have all the access in the world to go into these environments and learn as much as they want.

Last summer, the University of Michigan at Ann Arbor held a symposium on flow visualization and in Seattle, they hosted a conference on propulsions. Among the foreigners were two Czechoslovakians—they attended both, they knew both of these conferences were being held. One was stopped when he requested to go to a presentation on wind tunnels at the first conference.

I think the key point here is the awareness that these conferences exist and the locations and the openness of them certainly become a source for the Soviet Union and its bloc members to travel freely in the United States and gain access. No one monitors their conversations and the Americans often do not even recognize that they're being asked leading questions. . . .

Openness Threatens Security

In closing, I'd just like to bring it back to your world, and frankly, all of our worlds. What you're dealing with as librarians is the right to read and an open press. One might ask how far do we go or how far don't we go? What I've tried to do today in a short time—and hopefully, I haven't confused you too much—is to lay out the dilemma that we face: the technology that we use for peace, the Soviets want for defense. And as important as it is for us to have the technology we need to grow, to share, and to innovate, we have to look for that fine balance and understand that the controls are not meant to stop Americans from moving on, but that the Soviets use the same information for their defense and their aggressive acts.

"*Impeding that open communication among U.S. scientists and engineers which has helped bring this country to the forefront in science and engineering would significantly undermine . . . national security.*"

Technical Information Must Not Be Restricted

Stephen H. Unger

Stephen H. Unger is a professor of computer science at Columbia University in New York City. He is active in the Institute of Electrical and Electronics Engineers Society on Social Implications of Technology, and he has written a book called *Controlling Technology: Ethics and the Responsible Engineer*. He, like many scientists, recognizes the need for some control of information. But, as he states in the following viewpoint, he believes those restrictions should be very carefully designed so they won't harm security more than protect it.

As you read, consider the following questions:

1. Does Mr. Unger believe that the main reason for not heavily restricting scientific information should be the First Amendment?
2. What disadvantages does Mr. Unger see in overly restrictive policies?
3. What problems does Mr. Unger believe are a basic part of the censorship process?

Stephen H. Unger, "You Can't Have It Both Ways," *Bulletin of Atomic Scientists*, August/September 1983. Reprinted by permission of THE BULLETIN OF THE ATOMIC SCIENTISTS, a magazine of science and world affairs. Copyright © 1983 by the Educational Foundation for Nuclear Science, Chicago, IL 60637.

The campaign by government officials over the past half decade to clamp down on the free flow of scientific and technical information threatens fundamental principles of openness inherent in both the scientific process and in U.S. political traditions. A novel aspect of this campaign is the claim that the government should be able to impose secrecy on work done by private individuals or organizations not covered by contracts with secrecy provisions, and in some cases not involved at all with government contracts or grants. The issue is *not* the balancing of personal rights and privileges of individual engineers and scientists against the security of the nation. On the contrary, impeding that open communication among U.S. scientists and engineers which has helped bring this country to the forefront in science and engineering would significantly undermine the technological basis of the United States' national security.

In the political realm, the principles of free speech, freedom of the press and free assembly are justified mainly because they facilitate the efficient and just operation of society. Both in this area and in the scientific process, truth is most closely approached when ideas and data are exposed to an open process of criticism and enhancement. This stimulates the generation of new ideas and exposes errors, distortions and omissions. It also reduces the useless duplication of work.

Security Impaired by Secrecy

But isn't the security of the nation impaired when the results of U.S. research and development efforts are made available for exploitation by potential enemies? Why, for example, should we publish information useful to the Soviet Union in manufacturing integrated circuits incorporated in sophisticated weapons? Shouldn't we try at least to delay publication of such knowledge for a few years and make them expend the effort necessary to develop the information for themselves? Facile answers to these questions can be misleading. An outline of a deeper analysis yields a very different conclusion.

• There is no practical way to restrict the outflow of scientific and engineering knowledge across our borders without significantly reducing its availability within our borders.

• Restricting communications among members of a community is likely to impair their effectiveness to a far greater degree than would restricting their access to information generated elsewhere. This effect is enhanced by the fact that the technical publications of a country that is ahead in a given field are likely to deal principally with matters that will not be of concern to less advanced countries.

• It is argued that the restrictions on publication would not apply to basic ideas, but only to specific techniques that would facilitate actual production of devices and systems. But manufacturing know-how is not transferred effectively on pieces of paper. On-site training and the transfer of hardware are necessary for this purpose.

Openness Encourages Advances

In the context of current weaponry, incremental technological advances by the Soviet Union would not make any appreciable difference in the balance of power. But, in any event, a bottom-line argument is that the relatively open U.S. system has generated a lead of five to 10 years over the closed Soviet system in the fields of electronics and computers. Japan and some West European countries, who also follow relatively open publication policies, are also well ahead of the Soviet Union in these fields. In fact, a more restrictive U.S. policy would be largely nullified if a similar policy were not also adopted by these nations.

Acceptable Risk

The best way to ensure long-term national security lies in a strategy of "security by accomplishment," and an essential ingredient of technological accomplishment is open and free scientific communication. Such a policy involves risk, because new scientific findings will inevitably be conveyed to US adversaries. Nonetheless, the [National Academy] panel believes the risk is acceptable because American industrial and military institutions are able to develop new technology swiftly enough to give the US a continuing advantage over its military adversaries.

Dale Corson, *Physics Today,* February 1983.

It does not follow from the above arguments that nothing at all should be kept secret. Such matters as the details of military plans, cipher keys (but not the principles on which the ciphers are based), details of weapon designs and characteristics of systems related to electronic counter-measures ought to be safeguarded. This would not interfere significantly with engineering and scientific progress or with the discussion of issues of public interest.

One might at first be inclined to broaden this list to include more general characteristics of existing or proposed military systems. But this would make it impossible to have meaningful public debate over the wisdom of proceeding with the development and/or deployment of such systems as the MX missile, ABMs or cruise missiles. Existing secrecy now hampers discussion of matters such as the efficacy of verifying compliance with arms control measures via satellite observation or seismography. Certainly a vigorous public debate on the nuclear powered airplane project might have saved taxpayers a great deal of money. More discussion of the MIRVing of missiles when this idea was first proposed might have led to a more stable military situation. (And the concept of a missile with a single warhead would not now be the latest idea of strategic thinkers.) The events of recent decades make it clear that those charged with responsibility for national defense are by no means exempt from the human frailties that make us unwilling to allow those in other branches of government to conceal their operations from the public eye. Personal ambition, interservice rivalries, fanaticism, ignorance, corruption and stupidity have all shown a tendency to flourish behind screens labelled "national security."

Need for Clear Rules

Unless there are clear and narrowly drawn rules as to what may be kept secret, with strong oversight mechanisms, we can be sure that there will be major abuses. As far back as 1970, a Defense Department task force (chaired by Frederick Seitz and including Edward Teller) concluded that perhaps 90 percent of all classified scientific and technical information should be declassified. Their recommendations were not followed, and the report itself was classified.

During a period when an attempt is being made to persuade us that more secrecy is necessary, one might expect that particular care would be exercised as to the choice of cases. But even in this phase, we see one example after another of absurd behavior. Going back to 1977, there was the issuance of a secrecy order against three engineers planning to market a low-cost voice scrambler they had invented. During 1981, the State Department, which had set up an exchange program with the specific purpose of helping China in high technology areas, attempted to pressure several universities who had accepted students under this program into keeping them away from recent work in the computer area. This past November, the Air Force moved to block presentation at the Institute of Electrical and Electronics Engineers International Test Conference of three papers concerned with general techniques for making integrated digital circuits more testable. Although the work was done under an Air Force contract, it was not classified, was not particularly relevant to military systems and was of a nature quite similar to other work presented at the same conference or published elsewhere. After a minor furor, permission to present the papers was finally granted.

Typically Absurd Censorship

Such absurdities should not be regarded as perturbations in an otherwise reasonable system. They are typical examples of the way that censors behave. It is always safer for a censor to object to publication when there is any doubt. Since the criteria for rejection and the material being screened may both be difficult to comprehend, doubtful cases are likely to be common. When it may take an expert a full day to understand a typical paper, and where referees often disagree as to the merits of material they are reviewing for publication, what sort of staff can be set up to screen the many thousands of papers submitted monthly to U.S. journals and conferences? Who would take on such a job? A related point is that once it became known that work in a particular field was regarded as being particularly relevant to national security and thus more likely to be censored, researchers would naturally tend to avoid that field.

Crippling Obsession

An obsession with preventing leakage of our technology will cripple our ability to remain the leader.

Roland W. Schmitt, quoted in *Business Week*, June 4, 1984.

This discussion has focused on the problem of increased governmental constraints on the flow of scientific and engineering information. No implication is intended that there are not other serious barriers to this flow, such as commercial secrecy, the desire to beat out rival researchers, laziness and inadequate communications skills. The existence of some barriers in no way, however, justifies the imposition or tolerance of others.

"The implications of what . . . organized crime [has] learned from the FOIA [is] frightening; what hostile nations can learn poses a much greater danger."

The Freedom of Information Act Aids Society's Enemies

Francis J. McNamara

The Freedom of Information Act (FOIA), created in 1966, allows anyone in the nation to have access to any information possessed by the government if it is not deemed Top Secret for national security reasons. This includes data about individuals and organizations as well as product and technical information. Many critics of the FOIA, including Francis J. McNamara, believe that the FOIA causes more harm than good. Mr. McNamara served as executive secretary of the Subversive Activities Control Board and director of the House Committee on UnAmerican Activities. In the following viewpoint, he argues that, while FOIA sounds good in theory, in practice it assists criminals, terrorists, and spies.

As you read, consider the following questions:

1. List some of the ways Mr. McNamara says the FOIA harms law enforcement efforts.
2. What problems does Mr. McNamara see with the FOIA besides release of too much information to the wrong people?

Francis J. McNamara, "FOIA: A Good Law That Must Be Changed," *Human Events*, October 29, 1983. Reprinted with permission.

The Freedom of Information Act (FOIA), in many ways, is a highly desirable law. The Supreme Court itself has written approvingly of the freedom-preserving principles on which it is based.

FOIA's basic concept is that to preserve their free, representative government and the rights its Constitution confers on them, Americans must be informed about that government—what it is doing, how and why it is doing it. How can they vote intelligently if they are not so informed? How can they learn of inefficiency or corruption and act to eliminate them? How can they perform the many other duties of good citizenship? . . .

FOIA Dangers

It sounds great. But when practical applications of the law are examined, it becomes clear that there are very real dangers to Americans and the nation in it.

Why? Because as presently written, it fails to balance the government's right (i.e., the public's interest) in the confidentiality of certain material against any one individual's right to know—a right that is very clearly limited by the Constitution, the law and the general welfare.

Consider the case of Joanne Deborah Chesimard, also known as Assata Shakur:

In the pre-dawn hours of May 2, 1973, State Trooper James Harper pulled a car off the New Jersey Turnpike for speeding and radioed for a backup before approaching it. Trooper Werner Foerster responded and, while Harper talked to the driver at a patrol car (there was a license-registration discrepancy), spoke to the passengers. The one woman in the car pulled a gun and shot Foerster. . . .

It was not Chesimard's first violent crime. When the FBI, in September 1972, had issued a wanted poster for her based on her alleged participation (with five others) in a Queens, N.Y., gunpoint bank robbery in August 1971, the poster noted that one of her identifying marks was a gunshot wound scar on her abdomen. Only 25, she had already used seven aliases. And she was even known as the "soul" of the Black Liberation Army (BLA), a terrorist group that grew out of the Eldridge Cleaver faction of the Black Panther party and specialized in killing policemen. . . .

[Chesimard was indicted and imprisoned. In 1979 she escaped.]

FOIA Aids Terrorists

What does the FOIA have to do with this incident of revolutionary terrorist robbery, murder and cop-killing?

Authorities found in Chesimard's prison cell 327 documents totaling 1,700 pages of FBI information about herself and the BLA she had obtained by a simple FOIA request. She had been studying them before her escape.

The head of the New Jersey State Police, Col. Clinton Pagano, had an analysis made of the documents and sent copies of it to FBI Director William Webster and Atty. Gen. Benjamin Civiletti, in addition to personally calling Webster. Pagano's conclusion:

Chesimard not only learned the names of government informants from the documents, but "went to the very heart of the operations of the Bureau and other enforcement agencies. She learned our techniques; she learned how to anticipate what we would do."

Potential Threat to Security

It is amazing that a rational society tolerates the expense, the waste of resources, the potential injury to its own security which this F.O.I.A. process necessarily entails.

Federal Judge Gerhard Gessell, quoted in *American Bar Association Law and National Security Intelligence Report*, June 1983.

According to Webster, Pagano also told him that the knowledge Chesimard obtained from the FOIA papers impaired FBI and state efforts to apprehend her, that "without question, Joanne Chesimard has an in-depth knowledge of the procedures of your agency," and that "the working relationship between the New Jersey State Police and the FBI has suffered accordingly." . . .

FOIA Aids Criminals

Not only revolutionary killer terrorists, but organized crime and drug traffickers profit by the FOIA.

Gary Bowdach, who had spent his life in organized crime, and five years in the penitentiary, revealed that, while in prison, he had used the FOIA to find out whether the government had other investigations pending against him and in an effort to discover who had informed on him. He did not learn the identity of his informant, but believed he succeeded in learning who had informed on a friend—and passed on the information. What happened to the informant?

"I don't think the man is among the living anymore," he said. A "jailhouse lawyer," Bowdach filed FOIA requests with every government agency he thought would have a file on him—the FBI, IRS, Drug Enforcement Agency, U.S. Attorney's office, and Bureau of Alcohol, Tobacco and Firearms. He also filed requests for other convicts.

Oranized crime, he testified, made widespread use of the FOIA for the same reasons he had. He had no personal knowledge of informants identified and killed as a result of these requests, but believed the effort was very successful. "With these [organized crime] people, people tend to 'disappear,' " was the way he put it. . . .

Banking on Human Error

To capitalize on the human error element, Bowdach would sometimes file identical FOIA requests with the same agency several times—on the theory that one person would handle the first request, another the next one and, if he was lucky, each would make some error that would result in his getting information he should not have.

FBI officials have repeatedly confirmed Bowdach's testimony about extensive organized crime utilization of the FOIA to hamper law enforcement. Director Webster testified in 1982, for example, that organized crime elements in Detroit had earlier been instructed to file requests and that, as of the time he testified, the Bureau had received 38 in response to those orders. The list of requesters, he said, was "like a Who's Who in organized crime in Detroit." Their requests resulted in over 12,000 pages of FBI information on organized crime operations in that area being turned over to them.

Sixteen percent of FBI FOIA requests, it is estimated, come from prison inmates. The Drug Enforcement Agency gets 40 percent of its requests from convicted felons, many of them serving time when they file them.

The case of Philip Agee reveals another aspect of the dangers in the FOIA.

Since openly proclaiming his intention to destroy the CIA in 1974, Agee has worked diligently at that task via books (one written with the help of the Cuban Communist party), personal appearances, foreign travels and two publications, *CounterSpy* and *Covert Action Information Bulletin* (which Castro helped him launch). The Supreme Court has found that his activities threaten the security of this and other nations.

Agee—no dumbbell—filed an FOIA request with the CIA and other agencies in 1977, asking for all the information they had on him. Unsatisfied with their responses, he had his ACLU attorneys file FOIA suits for him in 1979 (he was then in Germany—after being expelled from England and other countries for his contacts with hostile intelligence agents).

His suit compelled the CIA to search for 8,699 documents in its files covered by his request. After carefully analyzing them, it refused to release 8,175 of them in their entirety, citing various FOIA exemptions—and gave him 524 in part only.

Incredible Expense

District Court Judge Gerhard Gesell upheld the CIA position in July 1981, ruling that its denials were justified (except for five letters from congressmen he ordered delivered to Agee on the ground that the FOIA did not protect them). Gesell commented as follows on the case in his decision:

"It is amazing that a rational society tolerates the expense, the waste of resources, the potential injury to its own security which this process necessarily entails."

He footnoted this concluding comment with these facts: The CIA, at the beginning of 1981, had spent 25,000 man-hours on Agee's request; the salaries involved totaled $327,715 and computer costs, $74,750. He added, "The costs now far exceed this sum."

And they will go far beyond Agee's CIA suit total. By the time his suits against the State and Justice departments, the FBI and the supersecret National Security Agency (NSA) are settled, the costs will be enormous.

F.O.I.A. Destroys Security Effectiveness

After Watergate there was an element of the death-wish in the readiness of legislators and media people to bow to the wishes of the subversives for fear of being thought illiberal. The outcome was two pieces of legislation—the Freedom of Information Act and the Privacy Act—that together made it impossible for the FBI, the Customs Service, and the police (as well as the CIA) to do their jobs properly. . . .

The Freedom of Information Act deprived the FBI (and the CIA) of the well-positioned agents who used to keep the Bureau (and the Agency) well informed.

Brian Crozier, *National Review*, May 27, 1983.

The congressional committee largely responsible for the 1974 amendments to the act which created the many dangers now inherent in it, estimated that those changes would cost only $50,000 the first year and $100,000 for each of the next five years. But FOIA now costs the government about $50 million a year. . . .

The implications of what Joanne Chesimard and her BLA, the RNA, WUO and organized crime have learned from the FOIA are frightening; what hostile nations can learn poses a much greater danger.

FOIA Aids Hostile Nations

The FBI knows that the KGB is using the FOIA to its advantage. The highest-ranking Soviet official to defect to the U.S., Arkady Shevchenko, former assistant secretary general of the United Nations, has stated that Soviet journalists have used

American "friends" to file FOIA requests for them—and it is a matter of public record that the Soviet news agency Tass (long used as a cover for spies), has filed FOIA requests with the State Department. Shevchenko has branded the FOIA as "stupid," because it gives Moscow information "on a golden plate."

Judge Antonin Scalia of the U.S. Court of Appeals has revealed that when he was assistant U.S. attorney general in the mid-70's, NASA was concerned because it was getting a "regular series" of FOIA requests from the Soviet trading company, Amtorg (which has been used for Soviet espionage since the 1930s). NASA officials contacted the Department of Justice to see if there was anything they could do to avoid supplying the information Amtorg asked for. The answer: "No." . . .

The human error element which Bowdach mentioned and counted on cannot be eliminated. Any person who has to sit all day long, day after day, endlessly screening thousands of pages of closely typed reports, inevitably becomes somewhat fuzzy-minded and makes errors. Moreover, there are other factors that make error certain.

FOIA requires that agencies respond to a request in 10 days and an appeal from a denial in 20—a time limitation no sensitive agency has been able to meet (all have been flooded with requests) and which has led to hundreds of suits. These suits remove control of the screening from the agency, turning it over to judges who too often have little appreciation of security needs. What happens then? . . .

Built-in Error Factors

There are other built-in error factors. The most expert CIA intelligence officer or FBI counterintelligence agent can never know how much the KGB or some other foreign intelligence agency knows about the situation or individual on which he is screening papers. He can therefore never tell whether or not information he is clearing for release will fill in some gap in its knowledge, providing it with extremely valuable information.

And how could anyone working on a huge release recall some little detail on page number 12 or 37 that just might tie in with some other details on pages 3,968 or 5,169 with the same result? And when, as is often the case, a number of people must work on a request, how can adequate cross-checking of such items be done?

Even the classification of documents does not protect adequately. In the Agee case, Judge Gesell noted that of the 8,699 documents found, 8,127 were classified and that 8,324 actually concerned CIA sources and methods (which must be protected at all costs). This means that 197 documents about sources and methods lacked the protection of classification. Moreover, seemingly nonsensitive information can be dangerously revealing. Gesell went to the CIA's headquarters to secretly inspect many of the documents at issue in the Agee case. He stated in his decision:

"Specific instances illustrating how readily identity of sources, for example, may be compromised by release of data not itself sensitive were noted by the Court during its *in camera* inspection."

Finally there is the fact that unqualified judges, arrogantly overruling the carefully considered judgments of concerned, highly professional intelligence-security officials, can order documents declassified—and have done so.

The international effects of FOIA are the same as the domestic and for the same reasons. Top officials of every U.S. intelligence agency—the CIA, NSA, DIA, DEA, FBI and State Department—have testified that FOIA is drying up their sources of information, that their ability to do their jobs and the security of the United States have been heavily damaged because of it. Those within the intelligence community fear that they, or their sources, will be compromised by its compelled revelations.

"The right of public access to the information of government is essential to democracy."

The Freedom of Information Act Aids the People

Diana Mtk Autin and The Campaign for Political Rights

The authors of the following viewpoint are among those who believe that the Freedom of Information Act (FOIA) is an essential guarantee of our nation's commitment to openness. Diana Mtk Autin, the author of Part I, is a lawyer and executive director of the Fund for Open Information and Accountability, Inc. The Campaign for Political Rights, the source of Part II, serves as a national network of individuals and organizations who promote government accountability and the right to dissent. In this viewpoint, the authors point out the importance of public access to government information, and they describe the safeguards that keep the FOIA from endangering public security.

As you read, consider the following questions:

1. According to Ms. Autin, why is it not surprising that the government is trying to make the FOIA more restrictive?
2. One criticism often leveled at the FOIA is its administrative costs; what do the authors of Part II say about this?
3. On what basis does the Campaign for Political Rights argue that the FOIA is not a threat to national security?

Diana Mtk Autin, "Securing Public Access to Vital Information," *engage/social action*, February 1984. Reprinted with permission.

"The Freedom of Information Act: Why It's Important and How to Use It," published in September 1982 by The Campaign for Political Rights in cooperation with The Center for National Security Studies. Reprinted with permission.

I

The right of public access to the information of government is essential to democracy. Without information, the ability of the public to play its part in public discussion, debate, and policy-making is severely limited.

Yet not until 1966 was this right guaranteed, through the passage of the Freedom of Information Act (FOIA). The FOIA was strengthened in 1974 as a result of the Watergate revelations of the consequences of secret, unaccountable government.

The files of the U.S. government contain a wealth of material on the decisions of every government agency, as well as data that private companies must file with the government. The FOIA has been the single most effective law ever passed in the struggle to secure public access to this information.

Vital Information Released

Vital information once hidden in agency files has been released under the Act, enabling the public to keep government agencies under control and responsive to citizen needs. The FOIA provides access to records compiled and possessed by any arm of the executive branch of the federal government, including all federal regulatory agencies and government-controlled corporations.

The law allows "any person," including the press, businesses, public interest groups, universities, and state and local governments, to request records. It also requires agencies to respond promptly to requests and sets specific time limits. It requires that any fees charged for search and copying must be reasonable, and orders agencies to reduce or waive fees if release of data primarily benefits the public.

Agencies are permitted, but not required, to withhold information if it falls within one of the nine specific exemptions spelled out in the law. Because the FOIA has a strong built-in presumption in favor of disclosure, courts have consistently held that the burden of proof rests on the agency attempting to withhold information, not on the requester.

The principal grounds for withholding records are the protection of national security information, confidentiality of sources, personal privacy, trade secrets, and other information specifically exempted under other statutes. If part of a record or document is exempt, the agency must delete that portion and release any segregable part.

Perhaps the most important fact about the FOIA is that it does not require a reason for requesting information. If a requester feels that an agency has not complied with the Act, she/he may appeal the agency's action administratively. An unsuccessful appeal may be challenged in federal court. . . .

FIRST, WE LAUNCH AN ALL-OUT ATTACK ON THE FREEDOM OF INFORMATION ACT...

THEN WE SEAL ALL LEAKS IN THE GOVERNMENT AND MAKE EMPLOYEES TAKE LIE —

DETECTOR TESTS, AND OATHS OF SECRECY COVERING FUTURE WRITING.

...WE'LL TELL YOU WHAT WE THINK YOU SHOULD KNOW ABOUT THINGS LIKE GRENADA.

WE'LL ALL BE A LOT BETTER OFF.

HAVE A NICE DAY!

Despite the usefulness of the FOIA as a tool for citizen initiative—or perhaps because of it—the current administration has targeted it for destruction.

At the center of the attack are proposed amendments to further exempt intelligence agency files, allow businesses to shield pollution, product safety, and worker health and safety data, lengthen the time agencies have to respond to requests, and increase fees to requesters. Although the worst package of amendments was defeated last year by organized public protest, the attempts continue.

In the last session of Congress, six backdoor amendments to the FOIA passed, including one exempting even *unclassified* information on nuclear energy from release. New legislation exempting operational files of the CIA has been unanimously passed by the Senate Intelligence Committee and will be considered by the full Senate when they return from winter recess.

These legislative attacks have been joined by numerous administrative actions. . . .

It is not surprising that these actions are occurring when the administration is facing protest over unpopular foreign and domestic policies. A government that knows its citizens want a healthy, clean environment, safe products and drugs, peace, and economic and social justice, will resist releasing information documenting its failure to meet those needs.

Now, when the threat to freedom of information is greatest, we must encourage the use of the FOIA in struggles for decent living and working conditions, an end to discrimination, and peace. In that way we can play our part in determining our nation's future.

II

Myth: The Freedom of Information Act is highly overrated—it has not really enabled citizens to participate more fully in government.

Reality: The volumes of books, articles and reports based all or in part on FOIA disclosures illustrate the tremendous value of the Act. While private citizens may not file as many FOIA requests as organizations, scholars and businesses, they have been the prime beneficiaries of many important FOIA disclosures obtained by organizations representing their interests. A recent study published by the Campaign for Political Rights, *Former Secrets: Government Records Made Public Through the Freedom of Information Act* lists 500 cases of how lawyers, business, journalists, consumers, state governments, historians and others have used the FOIA—and how the resulting disclosures have benefitted the public.

Myth: The FOIA costs too much for the government to administer.

Reality: Although the government has estimated that the FOIA costs approximately $50 million to administer, a detailed analysis of these costs has never been released. It is thus impossible to assess how much of the expense can be attributed to bureaucratic inefficiency and to costly agency attempts to withhold requested information.

Even if the government's estimate is accepted, the cost does not seem excessive compared to the millions of dollars the government spends on many other programs—or more importantly, when the benefits of the Act are considered. The FOIA has proven to be an invaluable check on excessive, wasteful government spending, and has actually saved the government millions of dollars. In addition, the FOIA has helped warn the public about unsafe products, thereby preventing untold numbers of injuries and deaths. . . .

The FOIA and National Security

Myth: The FOIA is a threat to the national security because it allows anyone—including KGB agents and unfriendly governments—to obtain access to sensitive information.

Reality: While foreign governments can request U.S. documents under the FOIA, U.S. officials are not compelled to give out or disclose sensitive government information. The Freedom of Information Act permits agencies to withhold documents if disclosure could "reasonably be expected" to endanger the national security or reveal intelligence sources or methods. Government agencies often invoke these exemptions, and there is no proof that information released under the FOIA has ever damaged the security of the nation.

The adequacy of the "national security" exemption is illustrated by the fact that agency decisions to withhold classified information have always been upheld by the courts. In fact, the CIA—the agency that most frequently criticizes the FOIA on national security grounds—has never been forced by a federal court to release records that its officials have insisted should be kept secret.

The FOIA and Law Enforcement

Myth: The FOIA has damaged federal law enforcement efforts by discouraging the cooperation of confidential sources.

Reality: The FOIA contains an exemption for investigatory records that have been compiled for law enforcement purposes; the law specifically exempts any records which, if released, would impede law enforcement, reveal confidential sources or disclose investigative techniques.

Strengthening Commitment to Debate

The Freedom of Information Act is one of the most important laws enacted by Congress. By making government information available to the public, the act strengthens America's commitment to informed, robust debate on all public policies.

Ira Glasser, *The Nation,* June 2, 1984.

In 1981, NBC News requested the FBI's own records on the FOIA to find out if the Act really was drying up FBI sources, as FBI Director William Webster had often asserted. According to the documents released to NBC, the FBI conducted an "impact study" from 1979 to 1980 totalling more than 2000 pages to demonstrate Webster's point. But Webster abruptly cancelled that study in 1980. It turns out that during the study, 7000 FBI agents across the country reported only nineteen instances in which potential informers were reluctant to or refused to divulge information because they feared their identities would be disclosed.

Myth: The FOIA makes it harder for the U.S. to get information from foreign intelligence agencies and governments.

Reality: The intelligence agencies have never been able to substantiate their claims that the FOIA has weakened their ability to get information from and cooperate with foreign governments. In fact, the CIA has admitted that it was not until its officials began arguing that the FOIA cannot guarantee confidentiality that foreign governments became hesitant to share information.

"The purpose of the Directive is to keep disclosure decisions in the hands of those who should bear responsibility for them."

Presidential Directive 84 Safeguards Security

Daniel B. Silver

Throughout his terms in office, President Ronald Reagan has been seriously concerned with the large number of information leaks made to the press. In March 1983 Mr. Reagan signed National Security Directive No. 84 which, among other things, required that all government employees with access to sensitive information sign a lifetime security agreement. Daniel B. Silver, a member of the Standing Committee on Law and National Security, served from 1979-1981 as general counsel of the Central Intelligence Agency. In the following viewpoint, Mr. Silver discusses the need for such a measure, arguing that it does not limit First Amendment rights.

As you read, consider the following questions:

1. Why does Mr. Silver believe that something like Presidential Directive 84 is needed?
2. According to Mr. Silver, why is it all right for the President to "leak" information that a lesser official would be criticized for?
3. How does Mr. Silver respond to criticisms that Directive 84 violates the First Amendment?

Daniel B. Silver, "Safeguarding National Security: A Defense of Reagan's Directive," *Intelligence Report*, June 1983. Reprinted by permission of the American Bar Association's Standing Committee on Law and National Security.

Unwarranted and exaggerated criticisms have been leveled at the president's new Directive on Safeguarding National Security Information which requires federal agencies to adopt policies governing contacts with the media, investigate unauthorized disclosures of classified military and intelligence secrets, permit the use of the polygraph in such investigations and in clearances, and, as a condition of access to classified information, make employees sign a non-disclosure agreement which, in the case of Sensitive Compartmented Information (SCI), must include a provision for prepublication review.

These moves, especially prepublication review, have been described inaccurately as an assault on the First Amendment and as a system of censorship which will inhibit former officials from speaking freely on topics of public interest. Such criticisms are implausible and ignore the serious need underlying the directive.

Widespread Leaking

"Leaking" classified military or intelligence secrets (materials whose intentional delivery to a foreign power could constitute espionage) has become endemic among lower-level government officials under administrations of both parties. The public is curiously complacent about this dangerous phenomenon. Yet, when a subordinate official leaks classified information—however lofty he may consider his motive—he is breaking the law and violating his oath of office. By putting personal ambitions or goals above the rule of law, the leaker undermines the Constitution, which establishes a government of laws, not men. Thus, in addition to impairing the nation's security against external threats, such leaks represent a serious internal breakdown in the discipline of constitutional government. One cannot tolerate, much less applaud (as some critics of the Directive appear to) official lawlessness in this context without risking its extension elsewhere.

Some have advanced the specious argument that leaks are justified because presidents and senior government officials also disclose secret information. Disclosure by the president, or another official who is authorized to make classification decisions, by definition cannot be unauthorized. If the disclosure is unwise, the president is accountable politically. The anonymous subordinate is not.

Directive's Purpose

The purpose of the Directive is to keep disclosure decisions in the hands of those who should bear responsibility for them. To the extent that, in the past, officials honestly may have thought in error that they were authorized to disclose classified information, the Directive now tells them that they are not.

Particular censure has been directed at prepublication review, on the ground that it will muzzle critics. These claims ring hollow when one considers several facts: First, the Directive covers, and under the law the government only can seek to prevent publication of, validly classified military or intelligence secrets—not political views. Second, it covers only those officials who have access to SCI, generally the most sensitive kind of intelligence secrets.

Third, the impact of such review is likely to be narrow, judging from the only existing model, the CIA's enforcement of its employee secrecy agreement. After the Supreme Court upheld that agreement in the *Snepp* case, the CIA published a policy excluding from prepublication review all public expression by former employees *"as long as [such expression] does not directly or impliedly constitute a statement of an informational nature about intelligence activities or substantive intelligence information."* As a result, a former CIA employee need submit only those writings in which he chooses to trade on "inside information" or to describe his intelligence exploits. This is a limited and reasonable requirement, certainly not massive censorship. Its impact on former CIA employees engaged in discussion of current events has been

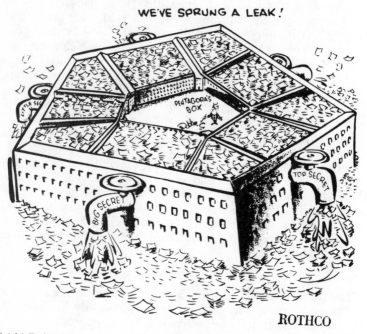

ROTHCO

slight, especially since the CIA completes time-sensitive reviews very quickly (even though court decisions allow 30 days).

These measures, taken by the CIA both to avoid inhibiting legitimate public discussion and to reduce the number of reviews, almost certainly will be adopted throughout the government under the Directive. Thus, there will be a minimal impact on public discussion by former officials.

Critics like the ACLU's Morton Halperin are wrong in describing the Directive as making a "mockery of the First Amendment"—an extraordinary assertion after the Supreme Court in *Snepp* upheld the same prepublication review against First Amendment attack. The First Amendment conceivably may protect the right of the press to receive classified information; it certainly does not guarantee that lawless officials can divulge it with impunity.

*"The Directive cannot help but have . . .
a devastating impact on informed public
discussion which is at the heart of our system
of democratic government."*

Presidential Directive 84 Destroys Freedom

Association of American Publishers

The Association of American Publishers (AAP) is a trade organization of book publishers which is strongly committed to the free
exchange of ideas and information as a vital part of the democratic process. Alarmed by President Reagan's Directive 84, the
AAP submitted testimony against it before two Congressional
subcommittees. The AAP was particularly concerned with the
Directive's requirement that all government employees with exposure to sensitive information be required, for their entire lifetime, to submit to prepublication clearance. That is, all materials, whether they be fiction or nonfiction, must be approved by
an appropriate government agency before they can be published. The AAP argues in the following viewpoint that this is a
direct assault on the First Amendment.

As you read, consider the following questions:

1. What does the author mean by "prior restraint"?
2. What evidence does the author cite to show that no security-
   endangering leaks would be prevented by Directive 84?
3. What damage does the AAP believe would be done by Directive 84?

Association of American Publishers, Inc., statement to subcommittees of the House of
Representatives on May 9, 1983.

There can be no doubt that Presidential Directive 84 is intended to be—and will operate as—a prior restraint on publication of enormous magnitude. As the writing of a distinguished constitutional scholar makes clear, a more classic prior restraint could not be found:

> The clearest form of prior restraint arises in those situations where the government limitation, expressed in statute, regulation, or otherwise, undertakes to prevent future publication or other communication without advance approval of an executive official. Such limitations are normally enforced by criminal prosecution for having published without the required approval, the prosecution being based upon mere failure to obtain approval and not on any issue concerning the content or manner of the publication. (Emerson, *The Doctrine of Prior Restraint.)*

The abhorrent nature of the Directive is not mitigated in the slightest by the fact that its enforcement takes the form of severe and confiscatory civil, as opposed to criminal, penalties.

Vast Impact

The scheme of prior restraint contemplated by the Directive is vast. The *minimum* procedures mandated by the Directive provide that all government employees with access to Sensitive Compartmented Information ("SCI") must sign an agreement which includes a provision for the prepublication review of their writings. While what is meant to be reviewed under this prepublication requirement is not spelled out in the Directive, as interpreted by the agency with the greatest familiarity with such procedures, the CIA, writings include not merely non-fictional works with respect to the subject of the author's government employment, but any books, including novels, as well as reports, studies, articles, columns, lecture notes, speeches, letters to the editor, book reviews, etc., which in any way relate to "intelligence data or activities." Further, review is mandated whether or not classified information is included in the writing, on the assumption that only the agency itself will be able to determine whether classified information would be disclosed by the publication.

The agreement which must be signed by individuals with access to SCI is not only binding with respect to writings produced by such persons while working for the government and having access to classified information, but also with respect to writings produced after they have severed any contact with the government and thus lost all access to classified information. . . .

Further, while the Justice Department has refused to reveal the numbers of individuals with SCI clearances, this provision clearly covers all of the government's highest officials and has been reported to apply to as many as 100,000 employees.

But, in addition, the prior restraint authority emanating from

Presidential seal

the Directive is not limited to the government's dealings with employees with access to SCI. The Directive provides that, in the individual agency's discretion, nondisclosure agreements to be signed by individuals with access merely to classified information may include a provision for prepublication clearance. By this provision, the potential reach of the prior restraint power has been expanded exponentially.

The prepublication review process contemplated by the Directive cannot help but have a pronounced chilling effect on the publishing process and a devastating impact on informed public discussion which is at the heart of our system of democratic government. . . . While every Administration has, at one time or another and to varying degrees, decried its inability to control unauthorized leaks, no previous Administration has gone so far in its efforts to ensure that the Executive Branch will control access to information. The reluctance of previous Administrations to take such drastic action may be accounted for by the fact that, despite periodic laments that unauthorized disclosures endanger national security and/or foreign relations, no specific harm from such disclosures has ever actually been identified. In this connection, Richard K. Willard, Deputy Assistant Attorney General and Chairman of the Interdepartmental Group which issued the Report on which the Directive is based, was asked in an interview on ABC's April 29, 1983 Nightline program to indicate how many unauthorized disclosures have caused harm each year. He responded that he did not know, asserting merely that "over the last decade [he is] sure that that has happened more than a handful of times."

More than ten years have passed since the Pentagon Papers were published over the Government's strenuous objections and despite its vigorous efforts to obtain a prepublication injunction on the ground that national security would be harmed by their public disclosure. In that time, nothing has validated the government's alarmist claims. It is evident that nothing more serious than embarrassment or political discomfort has resulted from that disclosure. On the other hand, the publishers of the Pentagon Papers made a powerful and important contribution to the education of the American people.

Needless Directive

This latest effort to shroud the government's activities in secrecy should be viewed with profound skepticism. There is no need for the Directive. Those who are determined to disclose information which truly may jeopardize the national security will not be deterred by this Directive. Indeed, such people are unlikely to take the time and trouble to write books. The broadly censorial impact of the Directive and the price that such Directive will exact on informed public debate fully warrants the conclusion that the Directive is alien to the free speech traditions of this country and both contrary and harmful to the First Amendment's "central" guarantee that "debate on public issues . . . be uninhibited, robust and wide-open." *New York Times Co.* v. *Sullivan,* (1964).

"The unauthorized disclosures of classified information . . . has become an increasingly common occurrence."

Security Leaks Must Be Stopped

American Bar Association Intelligence Report

Leaks of sensitive government information, both accidental and deliberate, have long been seen as a problem for those concerned with the nation's safety. The American Bar Association's Standing Committee on Law and National Security has devoted substantial portions of its newsletter, *Intelligence Report,* to this issue. The following viewpoint, taken from that newsletter, summarizes a report by a government interdepartmental committee. It recommended to President Ronald Reagan that strong preventive measures be taken to ensure that government employees will not indiscriminately disclose sensitive information.

As you read, consider the following questions:

1. What motives does the report suggest officials often have when they leak sensitive information?
2. What kinds of harm can result from the careless leaking of even non-secret information, according to the report?
3. What kinds of non-criminal penalties does the report recommend for officials who leak sensitive information?
4. Summarize the recommendations of the interdepartmental committee.

"Study Recommended Reagan's National Security Directive," *Intelligence Report,* June 1983. Reprinted by permission of the American Bar Association's Standing Committee on Law and National Security.

In early 1982, at the request of William B. Clark, assistant to the president for national security affairs, Attorney General William French Smith convened an interdepartmental group to study the effectiveness of existing statutes and Executive orders prohibiting unauthorized disclosure of classified information. The group was chaired by Deputy Assistant Attorney General Richard K. Willard and included representatives of the secretaries of State, Treasury, Defense and Energy, and the director of Central Intelligence. The group met throughout February and March of 1982; and on March 31, 1982, Attorney General Smith submitted a memorandum to the president which contained its findings and its recommendations. NSDD No. 84 closely follows the recommendations contained in the memorandum. But the report itself merits summarizing as a background document justifying the president's National Security Decision Directive. . . .

Examining the attitudes of officials who make unauthorized disclosures and of the journalists who print them, the report noted:

> Officials who make unauthorized disclosures may persuade themselves that they are serving the larger national interest by disclosing information that the public has a right to know. Such officials may seek to advance their personal policy objectives by leaks of classified information, on the assumption that there will be no serious harm to national security. Because leaks are so prevalent and leakers rarely caught, some officials may believe there is nothing wrong with leaking classified information and that everyone does it.
>
> Similarly, many journalists appear to believe they have a duty to divulge virtually any newsworthy secret information that can be acquired by whatever means they choose to employ. To their way of thinking, leaks are part of a game in which the government tries to keep information secret and the media tries to find it out. Some journalists are unwilling to assume responsibility for damage to the national security in situations where they win this "game."

Alarmingly Common Leaks

The unauthorized disclosures of classified information, said the report, has become an increasingly common occurrence and the severity of the problem has increased greatly over the past decade.

Speaking about the manifold harm done by such frequent unauthorized disclosures, the report said:

> —Particular items of information appearing in the press provide valuable intelligence for our adversaries concerning the capabilities and plans of the United States for national defense and foreign relations.
> —Unauthorized disclosures interfere with the ability of our government effectively to carry out its policies. This "veto by leak" phenomenon permits a single bureaucrat to thwart the ability of our democratic system of government to function properly.
> —Disclosures about U.S. intelligence programs are particularly damaging, because they may cause sources to dry up. Lives of human

121

agents are endangered and expensive technical systems become subject to countermeasures.

—In particular, foreign governments are reluctant to cooperate with the United States because we are unable to protect confidential information or relationships.

The problem, however, is not confined to classified leaks. "Some of the most embarrassing leaks," said the report, "do not involve classified information at all. We believe that leaks of classified information cause more serious and long-lasting damage, and thus warrant separate treatment as provided in this report. That is not to say that nothing can or should be done about leaks of unclassified information. The government is entitled to protect a variety of information from disclosure, including law enforcement investigatory information, proprietary data, predecisional memoranda and other information pertaining to internal government deliberations. Depending upon the circumstances, disclosure of such information may be unlawful, unethical, or a violation of applicable standards of conduct for government employees."

Criminal Penalties Needed

The report noted that the problem of unauthorized leaks has resisted efforts at solution under a number of administrations. While unauthorized leaks of classified information have been specifically prohibited by a series of Executive orders,

"They're buying a new six mainframe satellite-linked security system to try and stop the leaks."

© Punch/Rothco

There is no single statute that makes it a crime as such for a government employee to disclose classified information without authorization. With the exception of certain specialized categories of information, the government must ordinarily seek to prosecute unauthorized disclosures as violations of the Espionage Act or as the theft of government property. Such prosecutions have not been undertaken because of a variety of legal and practical problems.

Therefore, it would be helpful if Congress enacted a law providing criminal penalties for government employees who, without authorization, disclose information that is properly classified pursuant to statute or Executive order. Such a law would be appropriate in view of the substantial body of criminal statutes punishing unauthorized disclosure of other kinds of sensitive information by government employees, such as banking, agricultural and census data. Classified national security information deserves at least the same degree of protection.

In the paragraphs that follow we excerpt some of the other key passages from the report. . . .

Reluctant Investigations

Leaks of classified information constitute a potential violation of the espionage laws and other statutes that fall within the FBI's investigative jurisdiction. (By contrast, many agencies that originate classified information are not authorized to go beyond their own employees in investigating leaks.) However, the FBI has been reluctant to devote its resources to leak investigations. The burden of such investigations falls almost entirely on the Washington Field Office. Such investigations frequently involve high ranking government officials, who may be uncooperative. Sometimes a time-consuming investigation is undertaken, only to reveal that the source of the leak was a White House or Cabinet official who was authorized to disclose the information. Finally, it is very rare for an investigation to identify the leaking official, and even rarer that a prosecutable case is developed or that administrative action is taken against a leaker. . . .

In summary, the past approach to leak investigations has been almost totally unsuccessful and frustrating to all concerned. There have been frequent disputes between the Justice Department and agencies complaining about leaks. This ineffectual system has led to the belief that nothing can be done to stop leaks of classified information.

Unless new criminal legislation is enacted, we should recognize that leak investigations are unlikely to lead to successful criminal prosecutions. However, the present system would be greatly improved if employees who leak classified information could be identified and fired from their jobs. Therefore, we should recognize that the likely result of a successful leak investigation will be the imposition of administrative sanctions, except for cases in which exacerbating factors suggest that criminal prosecution should be considered. . . . When investigations identify employees who have disclosed classified information without authority, they should not be let off with a slap on the wrist. The full range of administrative sanctions—including discharge—is available. . . .

Summary of Recommendations

1. The administration should support new legislation to strengthen existing criminal statutes that prohibit the unauthorized disclosure of classified information.

2. All persons with authorized access to classified information should be required to sign secrecy agreements in a form enforceable in civil actions brought by the United States. For persons with access to the most sensitive kinds of classified information, these agreements should also include provisions for pre-publication review.

3. Agencies should adopt appropriate policies to govern contacts between media representatives and government officials, so as to reduce the opportunity for negligent or deliberate disclosures of classified information.

4. Each agency that originates or stores classified information should adopt internal procedures to ensure that unauthorized disclosures of classified information are effectively investigated and appropriate sanctions imposed for violations.

5. The Department of Justice, in consultation with affected agencies, should continue to determine whether FBI investigation of an unauthorized disclosure is warranted. The FBI should be permitted to investigate unauthorized disclosure of classified information under circumstances where the likely result of a successful investigation will be imposition of administrative sanctions rather than criminal prosecution.

6. Existing agency regulations should be modified to permit the use of polygraph examinations for government employees under carefully defined circumstances.

7. All agencies should be encouraged to place greater emphasis on protective security programs. Authorities for the federal personnel security program should be revised and updated.

To close the gaps in the present law, we recommend the introduction of legislation imposing a criminal penalty for all unauthorized disclosures of classified information by government employees. Such a statute should be simple and general in order to cover all situations, and might provide as follows:

Whoever, being an officer or employee of the United States or a person with authorized access to classified information, willfully discloses, or attempts to disclose, any classified information to a person who is not an officer or employee of the United States and who is not authorized to receive it shall be fined not more than $10,000, or imprisoned not more than three years, or both.

"Legitimizing the threat of the continuous government censor can only weaken free debate."

Free Speech Is More Important than Leaks

Lucas A. Powe Jr.

Lucas A. Powe Jr., Windfohr Professor of Law at the University of Texas, specializes in teaching about the First Amendment and constitutional law. He has done much writing about the First Amendment, focusing on the problems of mass communications. In the following viewpoint, he discusses the nature of censorship as being foreign to American values. He argues that the United States cannot fight a repressive enemy by imitating its censorious methods.

As you read, consider the following questions:

1. What are some of the reasons, according to Mr. Powe, that censorship "has a bad name in our society"?
2. According to Mr. Powe, how will Presidential Directive 84 affect the public debate of issues which is a vital part of a democratic society?
3. How does Mr. Powe resolve the apparent conflict when he says that, contrary to the views of censors, it is when the nation is greatly threatened that it is most important *not* to censor ideas?

Lucas A. Powe, Jr., "The Constitutional Implications of President Reagan's Censorship *Directive 84*," *The Center Magazine*, March/April 1984. Reprinted with permission from *The Center Magazine*, a publication of the Center for the Study of Democratic Institutions.

The Reagan Administration's *National Security Decision Directive 84,* the demand that all government officials having access to high-level classified information submit to government review all their manuscripts written for the general public, is an outrageous assault on the First Amendment. It is beyond precedent. It attacks the First Amendment at the very place where all First Amendment interests urge publication: i.e., someone wishes to engage in the public dialogue; large parts of the public wish to learn what the would-be speaker has to say; and the issue to be addressed is central to governmental policies.

It also attacks the First Amendment at the one place where there is no debate at all about what its framers intended: prior censorship should be unconstitutional. If government has the ability to punish individuals for what they said, the framers believed that that power could only be brought into play *after* the speech occurred. Licensing was totally forbidden.

Leaving both the history of the First Amendment and our subsequent traditions behind as relics of a simpler era, the Administration would relegate well over one hundred thousand government employees to the instant and permanent status of second-class citizens. If, after leaving government service, they wish to engage in debate on the major issues of the day with which they are most familiar, their abilities to do so would be limited. . . .

Why Censorship Is Bad

Since there cannot be a dispute that what is being proposed is a system of censorship, one would do well to recall exactly why censorship has a bad name in our society. First, much speech that could not be censored under any stretch of the imagination comes into the net of censorship. One need only pause for a moment on the requirement that prepublication review would be needed for any material containing any information regarding "intelligence activities." That phrase is, in turn, defined by reference to the President's Executive Order 12333 of December 8, 1981, and includes *everything* an agency is *authorized* to do, from the collecting of newspaper data, to the storing of information necessary for administrative purposes, to real intelligence activities. There is astonishing breadth in this system of censorship, and in order to flag the alleged "bad" speech, the censor must look through a lot of clearly protected speech. In turn, censorship delays speech. The article is ready for publication and then the censor begins formulating his decision as to whether and in what form it may be published. The control of the timing of the speech thus shifts from the speaker to the censor, at least within the limits set for a decision.

Next, there is a propensity toward an adverse decision about whether something may be published. Bluntly, a censor's job is to censor. In an Administration which sets up a massive program of censorship, which is unconcerned with the public's need for information and assumes that, if there is doubt, classify material at the highest possible level, is it likely that a censor will be reprimanded for censoring too much?

Censorship is also subject to political abuse. The CIA has previously admitted in congressional testimony that it has exercised its powers of censorship more heavily when the material to be censored is critical rather than supportive of the agency. One would hardly expect otherwise, no matter how piously the contrary is asserted. Such assertions are natural, and, not surprisingly, the Department of Justice has one such assertion in its statement.

Overprotection of Government

A system of censorship will thus overprotect the government by bringing materials that cannot be censored into its net, delaying their publication, and creating an incentive to over-censor.

Too Much Classification

Far too much government information is already classified—studies have shown that. I question the current efforts to intensify government secrecy when so much of what is secret is problematic. It would be very different if we could be sure that the government keeps only those secrets that are indispensable. . . .

Yet, because such a buildup of secrecy carries great dangers for any democracy, debate is indispensable. Instead of moving toward ever greater secrecy, I believe that this nation should honor its traditions of open government. We have been for the world a beacon of open government, and we have to be very careful not to squander that leadership.

Sissela Bok, *US News & World Report,* April 18, 1983.

But such a system has other insidious effects. Think for a moment of the would-be participant in public debate. He is an ex-official of the government. If the article he wishes to write will be critical of the administration in power, he knows that the censor will be more prone to be negative.

This is not the only deterrent, however. The would-be participant also knows that the censor will have a major impact on the timing of his, the speaker's, participation in the public debate.

Let me use a recent example. On August 28, the first two U.S. Marines were killed in Beirut. Suppose a prescient ex-official realized there would be an important debate on the War Powers Resolution and wished to write on that subject and influence the public debate. If he wrote the article instantly—i.e., in one day—but was subjected to the full thirty days of review before approval to publish was granted, then the article would first be available for publication on September 29, assuming that the review would not be stretched out over thirty working days. September 29 would be a full week after the Administration had, in fact, reached its compromise with congressional leaders, a day after the House of Representatives voted its approval of the compromise, and the same day the Senate voted. Thus the article, if published, would have been wholly irrelevant to the debate. The very system that creates an incentive for the government to censor creates a disincentive for ex-officials to try to participate in public debate in the first place.

A rule having such a direct effect in subjecting major participants in significant public issues to a regime of censorship prior to speaking is obviously foreign to our system. . . .

Proof of Need Is Lacking

My own view is that the case for this system of prior censorship cannot be made on any facts; it is foreign to our traditions and introduces the one thing the framers of the First Amendment intended to protect against—prior censorship. But for others who would allow a system of prior censorship, were a compelling need shown, I suggest that the Administration ought to bring forth the necessary data. If there is a compelling need, the Administration should be able to bring forth example after example and demonstrate the harm that has occurred to us. If the Administration will not do so—and its Report of the Interdepartmental Group on Unauthorized Disclosures of Classified Information does not even make a stab at attempting to show either need or harm—I suggest it is because it cannot do so. And if it cannot do so, then it has in fact substituted fear for both rational debate and the First Amendment.

The Constitution speaks to all of us: judges, legislators, lawyers, citizens. It is a short document, and while many of the phrases are delphic, a number are quite comprehensible. Freedom of speech is one of those comprehensible phrases. This is not to say that all First Amendment cases are easy to resolve. But it does suggest that there are many situations where anyone will know that the First Amendment speaks to the situation.

What is at stake here is one of those few situations where history, language, policy, and theory fairly leap out and shout that the First Amendment applies. If the First Amendment means that a knowledgeable public figure must obtain permission from the government in power before he may speak out in opposition to the government's policies in the area he knows best, then our Constitution is just like those of any number of closed societies: it reads well, but it lacks force when it matters. . . .

Ben Sargeant, *The Austin American Statesman*, reprinted with permission.

Legitimizing the threat of the continuous government censor can only weaken free debate. It can only make our Constitution appear, both in theory and in practice, like those of other lands where there is no pretense of freedom.

A system of government censorship has no place in American society. In the name of protecting the national interest, censorship protects mistakes; it protects those in power from the scrutiny their decisions merit; in essence, it "protects" the American people from the opportunity to make informed choices.

I concede that properly classified information ought not be divulged except through appropriate procedures. I agree that those persons with access to classified information owe a special obligation to all Americans not to abuse the trust that our government has placed in them. To the extent that the Administration is simply pursuing the end of protecting legitimate secrets, that is an appropriate goal.

But no matter how pure the goal is, there are some means that cannot be used consistent with our Constitution. A system of prior censorship is one of those forbidden means. It transfers from the people to the government the power to control both the content and timing of public debate. Our concept of a free society and open debate cannot tolerate such a transference. If the national interest is harmed by disclosure, then punish those who disclose. But do not punish all Americans by subjecting thousands of their fellow citizens to a regime of perpetual censorship.

A Mockery of Freedom

We simply cannot fight the world's closed societies by aping their methods. We made a mockery out of the First Amendment and destroyed countless lives and careers during the McCarthy era in the nineteen-fifties, a period when those in power concluded that the only way to fight Communists was to adopt tactics similar to those of the Communists, and that to protect our domestic freedoms, we had to curtail those freedoms.

It appears that the Reagan Administration has made a similar choice. In a fit of admiration for the way a closed society can control the range of information available to its citizens, the Administration seems intent on flattering those societies by imitating them.

There is a better model for our country. From Thomas Jefferson to Charles Evans Hughes to Hugo Black and William O. Douglas, it has been clear that the greater the perceived threat to our society, the more imperative it is to preserve our rights of freedom of expression "inviolate . . . in order to maintain the opportunity for free political discussion, to the end that government may be responsive to the will of the people and that changes, if desired, may be obtained by peaceful means. Therein lies the security of the Republic, the very foundation of constitutional government." (De Junge v. Oregon [1937], quoted in New York Times v. United States [1971]).

a critical thinking skill

Evaluating Censorship and National Security Concerns

In a democratic country there is a continual conflict between rights of individuals and the needs of the nation. One especially difficult area is that of national security. On one hand, Americans believe in complete openness and free access to the workings of the government. On the other hand, certain matters, if made public, could threaten the country's safety.

One example of this conflict came to light in 1979 when a college student wrote an article telling how to build an atomic bomb. He based his article on information he found in his college library. Subsequently, a furor arose when the article was published in a nationally distributed magazine. Alarmed officials said that publishing such information in a widely available source would make the atomic bomb possible for nations which previously had not had it and also would make it possible for terrorists and criminals to use the bomb. The editors of the magazine said that since the information was already publicly available, there was no reason not to publish it. Who was right—the magazine or its critics? Which was more important—free speech or national security?

In this activity, you will have a chance to examine your values in the area of censorship and national security.

Step 1

Below is a list of events that could occur. For each one, indicate whether you think it should be kept secret or should be public information. *If secret, put an S beside the event; if public, put a P.*

_____ a writer offers a magazine a story called "How to Build a Neutron Bomb in Your Basement"

_____ a person convicted of terrorism writes to the FOIA office requesting all information the government has collected about herself

_____ a government official holds a press conference about a "secret payload" on a satellite but requests that the reporters not print the information

_____ a reporter bribes a military official and finds out that secret maneuvers are going to take place on a small Caribbean island

_____ a person who was involved in a peaceful demonstration against an arms-building plant writes to the FOIA office requesting her files

_____ a paper detailing new methods of secret surveillance (spying) is going to be presented at a scientific conference

_____ a paper describing research about the effects of certain gases on humans is going to be presented at a scientific conference

_____ a newspaper has obtained a list of all US military officials, some undercover, in a Central American country

_____ a newspaper has obtained a list of all activities, both open and undercover, that the US armed forces participated in during World War II

_____ a newspaper has obtained a list of all activities, both open and undercover, that the US armed forces participated in during the past six years and up to the present

_____ a former CIA official writes a novel based very closely on the secret activities he has been involved in

_____ a computer slip-up allows secret information to get onto non-secret files; a government employee leaks the information to a reporter even though it was obviously intended to be secret

_____ a directive has been drafted by the State Department preventing tourists from certain countries such as the Soviet Union from visiting any area in the US which has military installations

_____ an African refugee is willing to give an interview detailing the secret methods US military personnel have taught his people to use against communists

_____ a low-level clerk in the defense department who files non-secret papers, answers telephones, etc. has been asked to sign a life-time secrecy agreement

_____ a magazine has obtained a secret government report indicating that a strategic nuclear reactor does not meet safety standards and if not repaired within a short time may endanger the lives of the people who work there and who live nearby

_____ a radical newspaper has obtained a list of access codes for US military computers

If you are a member of a class, discuss your answers in a small group. If you are doing this activity alone, you may want to ask someone to discuss it with you. This may lead to valuable insights about your own values regarding the First Amendment and national security. It may also expose you to significant ideas you had not thought of when you made your initial evaluation of these events.

Step 2

What criteria did you use to determine whether information should be public or secret? Below is a list of possible factors. Look the list over and add any other factors that influenced you in Step 1.

Now rank these factors: Number 1 for most important, 2 for next in importance, and so on until all of the factors are ranked.

_____ Free access to information is essential in a democracy.

_____ National security is essential to any country.

_____ Criminals do not have the same rights as other citizens.

_____ Some government "secrets" are not really very important to our security.

_____ Free exchange of information aids development of science and technology

_____ Lives should not be threatened by exposing secret information in the name of free speech.

_____ Lives should not be threatened by withholding information in the name of national security

_____ The rights of individuals should be safe-guarded no matter what the price.

_____ The good of the nation must be considered above all other factors.

_____ Other factors:

If you are working in a class, compare your rankings with others in the class. Try to reach a group consensus.

Also consider whether your values coincide with the interests of the nation at large.

Step 3

Reflect on the events described in Step 1 and on your own values as considered in Step II.

Then write a brief statement outlining policy for dealing with the censorship/national security conflict: What should be the determining factors editors or government officials use when deciding whether information affecting national security should be kept secret or made public?

Periodical Bibliography

The following list of periodical articles deals with the subject matter of this chapter.

Floyd Abrams — "The New Effort to Control Information," *The New York Times Magazine*, September 25, 1983.

Allan Adler — "Unclassified Secrets," *Bulletin of the Atomic Scientists*, March 1985.

Business Week — "Technology Transfer: A Policy Nightmare," April 4, 1983.

Rosemary Chalk — "Security and Scientific Communication," *Bulletin of the Atomic Scientists*, August/September 1983.

Henry Eason — "Defending Defense Secrets," *Nation's Business*, December 1983.

Constance Holden — "Historians Deplore Classification Rules," *Science*, December 16, 1983.

Guenter Lewy — "Can Democracy Keep Secrets?" *Policy Review*, Fall 1983.

Tony Mauro — "When the Government Gives Away Companies' Trade Secrets," *Nation's Business*, November 1983.

Melvyn B. Nathanson — "Academic Freedom Versus Nonproliferation: the Libyan Case," *Bulletin of the Atomic Scientists*, March 1985.

The Nation — "The A.C.L.U. and the F.O.I.A. Bill," June 30, 1984.

The New Republic — "Leaky Liberties," April 25, 1983.

Aric Press with Diane Camper — "Keeping the Cats in the Bag," *Time*, April 18, 1983.

Richard Schmidt — "Government Secrecy," *Newsletter on Intellectual Freedom*, September 1984. Available from American Library Association Intellectual Committee, 50 East Huron Street, Chicago, IL 60611.

Lois P. Sheinfeld — "Washington vs. the Right to Know," *The Nation*, April 13, 1985.

Dale Van Atta — "The Death of the State Secret," *The New Republic*, February 18, 1985.

Is School and Library Censorship Justified?

Chapter Preface

Should school children and the general public be protected from offensive or subversive materials, or should such materials be widely available in public schools and libraries? This question has probably been debated as long as schools and libraries have existed. Many people feel that since selection has to be made anyway, teachers and librarians have a responsibility to select only the most uplifting materials. Others believe that in a democracy, where traditionally all ideas are debatable, a wide range of materials on all points of view should be available to the public. Many also believe that schools, where young people are under the intellectual guidance of responsible adults, are the perfect place to expose them to dissenting opinions.

Both the general content and the perspective of school and library materials is at issue. The viewpoints in this chapter debate whether the views of particular segments of society should, for the general good, be allowed to dominate materials acquired with taxpayers' money.

"If the school board or the library board does not reflect the values of the citizens in the area of its jurisdiction, the voters have the right to change."

Libraries Should Reflect Majority Values

Phyllis Schlafly

Phyllis Schlafly, a highly energetic, conservative political activist, is best known for her campaign against the Equal Rights Amendment. She is a strong defender of traditional family and religious values. In the following viewpoint, she points out the necessity for those who spend taxpayers' money (specifically, teachers and librarians) to be accountable for how they spend it. The very fact that selection is necessary, Mrs. Schlafly says, causes a kind of pre-censorship. Therefore it is essential that those with selection-power be accountable to the values of those who pay the bills.

As you read, consider the following questions:

1. Why does Mrs. Schlafly think that library and school materials must reflect the values of the people they serve?
2. Does Mrs. Schlafly advocate eliminating all materials which may not agree with the values of the majority?

"Citizens' Bill of Rights about Schools and Libraries," *The Phyllis Schlafly Report*, February 1983. Reprinted by permission.

138

1. All those who spend taxpayers' money are accountable to the public. (The "public" includes citizens, parents, private groups, and the media.) The public has a right to exercise its right of free speech on how taxpayers' funds are spent and on what standards, to second-guess the judgment of the persons doing the spending, and to remove from office those responsible for any misuse of tax funds. Public supervision and criticism may be annoying, but they must be endured by all those spending tax funds, whether they be Presidents, Congressmen, bureaucrats, military, teachers, librarians, or others.

2. Since parents have the primary responsibility for the education of their own children, schools should have a decent respect for the parents' beliefs and attitudes. Schools should make every possible effort to avoid offending the religious, ethical, cultural or ethnic values of school children and their parents. Since presumably all educators would agree that *Playboy* and *Penthouse* magazines are not suitable reading materials for school children, it is clear that the issue over any particular book is one of appropriateness (which is a value judgment), not the First Amendment or "academic freedom."

Make Requirements Flexible

3. Since thousands of good books and hundreds of important, educational books are easily available, and since a child can read only a small number of books prior to high school graduation, it is highly unreasonable and intolerant for a school or teacher to force a child to read a particular book as a precondition to graduation or to passing a course. When a book selected as course material or supplementary reading offends the religious, ethical, cultural or ethnic values of a child or his parents, an alternate book should be assigned or recommended which does not so offend. This substitution should be made without embarrassing the child.

4. This same respect for parental values and the assignment of alternate books should apply when the question is raised as to the assignment of a book at a particular grade level. Many books are appropriate in the upper grades which are not at all appropriate for younger children. Parental decisions about the maturity of their own children should be respected by the schools without embarrassing the child.

5. Public libraries should adhere to a standard like the Fairness Doctrine which governs television and radio broadcasters; i.e., they have the obligation to seek out and make available books on all sides of controversial issues of public importance. For example, libraries should present a balanced selection of book titles on sensitive current issues such as the morality of nuclear war, women's liberation, basic education, evolution/creationism, Reaganomics, and the Equal Rights Amendment.

6. Child pornography (i.e., the use of children in pictures, books or films to perform sex acts or to pose in lewd positions or circumstances) should be absolutely prohibited. In 1982, the U.S. Supreme Court held in *New York v. Ferber* that child pornography is not protected by the First Amendment because the prevention of sexual abuse of children is "a governmental objective of surpassing importance." Laws against child pornography, therefore, must apply equally to everyone including bookstores, theaters, schools, and libraries.

7. No library buys every book published. Every day in the week, librarians, teachers and school administrators are making decisions to select some books for library shelves and school classrooms while excluding (censoring) other books. These select-and-exclude decisions can be called "preemptive censorship."

Important Responsibility

The selection of reading materials is a major responsibility of school and library personnel. Most such personnel have the historical knowledge, fairness, and mature judgment which are necessary to make those decisions. However, the public always has the right to question whether any preemptive censorship is carried out on the basis of the personal political biases of the librarian or teacher, or results from a genuine attempt to give students and the public the wisdom of the ages through time-tested "great books" plus fairness on current controversies.

The public clearly has a First Amendment right to investigate, evaluate and critique the selections and the criteria. If the school board or the library board does not reflect the values of the citizens in the area of its jurisdiction, the voters have the right to change the board members through the political process. That's an important part of our free, democratic society.

"It is in the public interest for publishers and librarians to make available the widest diversity of views and expressions."

Libraries Should Reflect Diverse Views

American Library Association

The American Library Association (ALA) has long believed that it is the responsibility of libraries to furnish to the public the widest possible range of materials. A constant concern is the pressure groups which attempt to impose their own values on library selection. The following viewpoint, taken from the ALA's "Freedom to Read Statement," reflects its views.

As you read, consider the following questions:

1. Why does the ALA believe that it is essential to provide a wide range of materials even though some may directly oppose majority values?
2. What does the ALA statement say librarians should do when faced with pressure by individuals or groups to censor materials?
3. Does this ALA statement offer any selection guidelines at all, or does it suggest that *all* materials have equal validity in a library?

American Library Association, "Freedom to Read Statement," adopted June 25, 1953; revised January 28, 1972.

The freedom to read is guaranteed by the Constitution. Those with faith in free men will stand firm on these constitutional guarantees of essential rights and will exercise the responsibilities that accompany these rights. We therefore affirm these propositions:

1. It is in the public interest for publishers and librarians to make available the widest diversity of views and expressions, including those which are unorthodox or unpopular with the majority.

Creative thought is by definition new, and what is new is different. The bearer of every new thought is a rebel until his idea is refined and tested. Totalitarian systems attempt to maintain themselves in power by the ruthless suppression of any concept which challenges the established orthodoxy. The power of a democratic system to adapt to change is vastly strengthened by the freedom of its citizens to choose widely from among conflicting opinions offered freely to them. To stifle every nonconformist idea at birth would mark the end of the democratic process. Furthermore, only through the constant activity of weighing and selecting can the democratic mind attain the strength demanded by times like these. We need to know not only what we believe but why we believe it.

2. Publishers, librarians, and booksellers do not need to endorse every idea or presentation contained in the books they make available. It would conflict with the public interest for them to establish their own political, moral, or aesthetic views as a standard for determining what books should be published or circulated.

Publishers and librarians serve the educational process by helping to make available knowledge and ideas required for the growth of the mind and the increase of learning. They do not foster education by imposing as mentors the patterns of their own thought. The people should have the freedom to read and consider a broader range of ideas than those that may be held by any single librarian or publisher or government or church. It is wrong that what one man can read should be confined to what another thinks proper.

Impersonal Evaluation of Books

3. It is contrary to the public interest for publishers or librarians to determine the acceptability of a book on the basis of the personal history or political affiliations of the author.

A book should be judged as a book. No art or literature can flourish if it is to be measured by the political views or private lives of its creators. No society of free men can flourish which draws up lists of writers to whom it will not listen, whatever they may have to say.

4. There is no place in our society for efforts to coerce the taste of others, to confine adults to the reading matter deemed

Copyright, 1982 USA TODAY. Reprinted with permission.

suitable for adolescents, or to inhibit the efforts of writers to achieve artistic expression.

To some, much of modern literature is shocking. But is not much of life itself shocking? We cut off literature at the source if we prevent writers from dealing with the stuff of life. Parents and teachers have a responsibility to prepare the young to meet the diversity of experiences in life to which they will be exposed, as they have a responsibility to help them learn to think critically for themselves. These are affirmative responsibilities, not to be discharged simply by preventing them from reading works for which they are not yet prepared. In these matters taste differs, and taste cannot be legislated; nor can machinery be devised

143

which will suit the demands of one group without limiting the freedom of others.

5. It is not in the public interest to force a reader to accept with any book the prejudgment of a label characterizing the book or author as subversive or dangerous.

The idea of labeling presupposes the existence of individuals or groups with wisdom to determine by authority what is good or bad for the citizen. It presupposes that each individual must be directed in making up his mind about the ideas he examines. But Americans do not need others to do their thinking for them.

Encroachments on Freedom

6. It is the responsibility of publishers and librarians, as guardians of the people's freedom to read, to contest encroachments upon that freedom by individuals or groups seeking to impose their own standards or tastes upon the community at large.

It is inevitable in the give and take of the democratic process that the political, the moral, or the aesthetic concepts of an individual or group will occasionally collide with those of another individual or group. In a free society each individual is free to determine for himself what he wishes to read, and each group is free to determine what it will recommend to its freely associated members. But no group has the right to take the law into its own hands, and to impose its own concept of poltics or morality upon other members of a democratic society. Freedom is no freedom if it is accorded only to the accepted and the inoffensive.

7. It is the responsibility of publishers and librarians to give full meaning to the freedom to read by providing books that enrich the quality and diversity of thought and expression. By the exercise of this affirmative responsibility, bookmen can demonstrate that the answer to a bad book is a good one, the answer to a bad idea is a good one.

The freedom to read is of little consequence when expended on the trivial; it is frustrated when the reader cannot obtain matter fit for his purpose. What is needed is not only the absence of restraint, but the positive provision of opportunity for the people to read the best that has been thought and said. Books are the major channel by which the intellectual inheritance is handed down, and the principal means of its testing and growth. The defense of their freedom and integrity, and the enlargement of their service to society, requires of all bookmen the utmost of their faculties, and deserves of all citizens the fullest of their support.

"What we are dealing with is a group of crazies ready to go to the wall to keep your child from thinking."

Censorship by the Religious Right Undermines Education

Michael Scott Cain

Some individuals believe that exposure in school to as many ideas as possible will enrich a child's education and encourage independent thinking. Others argue that what children are taught should reflect the values of their elders and that to present them with alternative concepts will either confuse or corrupt them. Michael Scott Cain, an English teacher at Catonsville Community College in Catonsville, Maryland, is appalled by those who seek to "shelter" children from views unlike their own. He is particularly concerned about the influence of the "radical religious right" which, he says, seeks to remove from the curriculum all ideas with which it doesn't agree.

As you read, consider the following questions:

1. Why is Mr. Cain so deeply concerned about the actions of the "radical religious right"?
2. Mr. Cain says that the religious right is not so much concerned with *books* as with the philosophy of "secular humanism." According to Mr. Cain, how does the religious right define secular humanism?
3. Does he agree that secular humanism is a threatening concept? Why or why not?

Michael Scott Cain, "Crazies at the Gate: The Religious Right and the Schools." This article first appeared in THE HUMANIST issue of July/August 1983 and is reprinted by permission.

145

As I write this, an *American Heritage Dictionary* rests on the desk in front of me. If I were a school-aged child in Anchorage, Alaska, I would be denied that dictionary. It has been banned from the schools.

Why? Because a group called People for Better Education complained about it and demanded its removal. The group objected to the listing of such "obscene" words as *bed, tail, ball,* and *nut.*

The situation sounds ludicrous, just another example of the rampant lunacy that periodically breaks loose in our nation. If it were an isolated incident we could, provided we did not live in Anchorage, laugh at it. But ludicrous as it is, the incident is in no way isolated. The dictionary has also been banned in Cedar Lake, Indiana, and Eldon, Missouri. In the state of Texas, not only is the *American Heritage* banned but students are also forbidden access to the *Doubleday Dictionary, The Random House College Dictionary* (revised edition), *Webster's New World Dictionary of the American Language* (college edition), and *Webster's Seventh New Collegiate Dictionary.*

The objections Texans raised to these books are every bit as silly as those raised in Anchorage by the People for Better Education.

Bannings and Burnings

But dictionaries are not the only books coming under fire today. All over this nation, adults are joining together into well-organized groups in order to decide what children can—and cannot—read in schools. Bannings and burnings are taking place in virtually every state. The radical religious right, having discovered its political muscle, is taking on the schools. . . .

Censorship, book bannings and burnings, and attempts to control the thinking of others have been with us since religious bigots, thrown out of Europe, set up shop in New England. Silencing the opposition through intimidation is a tactic that goes back as far as the Salem witch trials. But our most recent wave of incidents probably has its roots in the battle for the minds of the children of Kawaha County, West Virginia.

When I was a child, I lived for a time in Charleston, the Kawaha County seat, the site of many book battles. I remember it as a pleasant place where people greeted you with a smile and a wave, a place where the idea of community had meaning. Later, during my college years, I hitchhiked through there. An elderly couple, local residents, picked me up, insisted I share their picnic lunch, and drove me a dozen miles out of their way to make sure that I wouldn't get caught in a spot where it would be difficult to get another ride. So when schools and buses were firebombed there, when people were shot and beaten, all in a dispute over what could be read in the schools, I was, to say the least, startled.

To discover how that could happen in Charleston, a fairly progressive and generous-hearted city, we have to ask who was responsible. Was there a key person who can shoulder the blame? Although she was far from the only person involved, a school board member named Alice Moore draws the lion's share of shame. Just as the Civil War was often called Mrs. Stowe's War, the battle of Charleston can be called Mrs. Moore's.

Mrs. Moore's war began when local teachers were asked to draw up a list of 325 language arts texts that they felt should be used in the schools. The teachers submitted the list to the school board, which voted unanimously to approve it. However, the board decided not to appropriate the money until the list could be studied in more detail.

Moore decided to do the studying and got in touch with Mel and Norma Gabler for help. The Gablers are professional censors from Texas who have successfully kept texts out of schools in their state, banned the previously mentioned dictionaries, and sent shock waves through the publishing industry by demanding editorial control over books used in the state schools. They publish reviews of texts and frequently help organize censorship efforts in other states. Members of the religious right, the Gablers object to books that promote negative thinking, display inappropriate values, lack patriotism, and show white people in an unfavorable light, among other things. They sent copies of their reviews of the approved books to Moore. The fact that they had not read many of the books on the list didn't slow them down at

Michael Keefe for the Denver Post, reprinted with permission.

all—you don't have to eat the whole apple to know it's bad.

The Gablers' reviews, naturally enough, demonstrated that the books in question were hotbeds of secular humanism, disrespectful of authority and religion, destructive to social and community values, obscene, pornographic, and unpatriotic.

The Devil's Work

The wife of a self-ordained minister, Moore knew the work of the devil when she saw it. These books had to die, so she made moves to kill them. The religious community joined the war first: ten ministers lined up to oppose Moore, while twenty-seven joined her ranks. The congregations followed their leaders, and at the next school board meeting over a thousand persons showed up to watch the board deny eight of the contested books. But the board approved the rest. Moore knew that wars weren't won on partial victories; she went home to sharpen her saber.

The war continued through the summer. Among the casualties were the works of Kurt Vonnegut, Richard Brautigan, Bernard Malamud, Wordsworth, the author of Ecclesiastes, Winston Churchill, Richard Wright, and Elizabeth Barrett Browning.

By September, the board knew it was outgunned. It voted to have the books reviewed by a citizen's committee, an act comparable to letting an armed mortal enemy loose on prisoners of war. The books were removed from the schools for a thirty-day examination period.

Demand for Bans

After the board capitulated, hell broke loose in Charleston. High school students walked out in protest of the decision. The right, sensing an advantage while the enemy was confused, set up pickets and demanded that the books be burned. A man protesting the pickets was shot. Soon after, a second anti-book-burner was shot and another bibliophile was savagely beaten—both men wound up hospitalized.

Hoping to restore order, the superintendent closed the schools for a cooling-off period. The tactic didn't work. The day he reopened them, eleven men—three of them ministers—were arrested for violating a court order concerning the number of pickets allowed at a single location. One minister publicly demonstrated Christian charity by praying for the deaths of three school board members who supported the disputed books.

As the violence continued to rise and the people of Charleston suffered more shootings, bombings, beatings, and arrests, the school board caved in entirely. Amid cheers from the right, the board voted to ban the books. Shortly thereafter, amid more cheers, the school superintendent resigned.

After Alice Moore's war, the incidence of book burnings rose all over the nation, bearing all the earmarks of an organized campaign by the religious right. As two New York City mayors have pointed out, no one was ever harmed by a book. Why, then, is the radical right so anxious to restrict access to ideas? Why do they insist on determining which books your children can read?

Secular Humanism

Actually, books are not the issue. Books are burned and banned because of the philosophy the right says those books expound, the code they find particularly noxious: secular humanism.

Secular humanism is a code word that has almost replaced communism in the right's vocabulary. What it means precisely is hard to determine; we could say that it refers to anything of which the right disapproves. . . .

Censorship Against Conspiracy

Don Cameron, executive director of the National Education Assn., the national teachers' union, said the worry over secular humanism in schools is the product of conservative "extremists" who have become "more strident in their promulgation of this notion in the last two or three years since the Reagan Administration took office."

"They take a string here, a twig there and build a nest of intrigue linked to the devil and communism," Cameron said in an interview. "They see a conspiracy to brainwash children and send them all to hell. It's crazy. It's crazy stuff."

Peter J. Boyer, *Los Angeles Times*, November 11, 1984.

According to the right, secular humanism is the reason behind falling test scores, declining values, lack of Christian morals, poor grammar (although their own publications are riddled with fractured sentences and mangled grammar), situational ethics, and the rest of the horrors to which they object. It is the force that is destroying the family, wrecking society, and wiping out the minds of children.

Who are these secular humanists? In order to help others identify the enemy, the National Congress for Educational Excellence has compiled a list of key words and phrases that godless humanists often use. If any of these words are in your vocabulary, you are probably a secular humanist: *academic freedom, analysis, career education, creative writing, human growth, identity, parenting, racism, world view, self-understanding.* There are over three hundred words on the list, but most of them are not needed. The ten listed above cover most of the human race.

If you qualify as a secular humanist, you are a member of a

vast conspiracy against America. You are probably also considered a communist and should not be allowed to have any say in what goes on in our schools—either as a teacher, staff member, or parent.

Divine Crusade

The right sees the removal of secular humanism from the schools as a divine mission, a crusade. . . .

The basic premise is that a vast conspiracy of secular humanists is out to wrest control of this nation away from the good Christian people. A single act might appear, to us, innocent; but if you see the totality, the big picture, as they do, then you will recognize godless humanism at work. Accept their premises, and evidence abounds: each child who does not read and write at grade level becomes the victim of a conspiracy; each school that tries to develop values becomes a thrusting edge of the plot. . . .

What we are dealing with is a group of crazies ready to go to the wall to keep your child from thinking, a group certain that they are acting in the child's own good. . . .

As Richard Hochstader writes in his book *The Paranoid Style in American Politics:*

Since what is at stake is always a conflict between absolute good and absolute evil, the quality needed is not a willingness to compromise but the will to fight things out to a finish. Nothing but complete victory will do. Since the enemy is thought of as being totally evil and totally unappeasable, he must be totally eliminated—if not from the world, at least from the theater of operations to which the paranoid directs his attention.

No Neutral Parties

The theater of operations is now our schools, and, since we do not fully realize we are at war, we are losing. If we wish our schools to survive, we must realize who we are in the eyes of our enemies. I use the word *we* deliberately because, for the radical right, there are no neutral parties; those who are not with them are members of the conspiracy.

*"Basic values . . . have for the most part,
been censored from today's public-classroom
textbooks."*

The Religious Right Must Guard American Values

Jerry Falwell

The Reverend Jerry Falwell, founder of the influential Moral Majority, Inc., is deeply concerned that America's traditional values are being undermined by those who remove God from all public institutions, including schools. In the following viewpoint, he writes that humanist educators teach that all values are relative; that is, there is no absolute right or wrong. This false concept, according to Mr. Falwell, threatens the stability of the nation. It is up to parents to fight the treacherous indoctrination of their children.

As you read, consider the following questions:

1. According to Mr. Falwell, what has changed in American education in the past thirty years?
2. What are some of the examples Mr. Falwell gives of dangerous concepts taught in schools?
3. Why, according to Mr. Falwell, are parents often unaware of the kinds of things their children are being taught?

Excerpt from LISTEN AMERICA! by Jerry Falwell. Copyright © 1980 by Jerry Falwell. Reprinted by permission of Doubleday & Company, Inc.

In his inaugural address on March 4, 1797, John Adams, our second President, stated that one means of preserving our Constitution was to "patronize every rational effort to encourage schools, colleges, universities, academies, and every institution for propagating knowledge, virtue, and religion among all classes of the people." He spoke of the high destiny of this country and of his own duties toward it, having been "founded on a knowledge of the moral principles and intellectual improvements of the people deeply engraved on my mind in early life." When John Adams graduated from Harvard, its handbook for "rules and precepts" stated: "Let every student be plainly instructed and earnestly pressed to consider well the main end of this life and studies is to know God, and Jesus Christ, which is eternal life. And therefore to lay Christ in the bottom as the only foundation of all sound knowledge and learning."

Our Founding Fathers knew the importance of education. They consider it a privilege of free men to be educated and to perpetuate their freedom by teaching the religious principles upon which our republic was built. When John Adams was President he said, "So great is my veneration for the Bible that the earlier my children begin to read it, the more confident will be my hope that they will prove useful citizens of their country and respectable members of society."

Education Passes On Society's Values

D. Bruce Lockerbie says in his recently published book *Who Educates Your Child?*: "Education is a framework like the forms that hold molten lead or liquid concrete, helping to mold character. Education is a mirror to reflect the development of that character. In other words, education is the instrument for carrying out society's philosophical goals."

In the past, parents did not have to worry about the education of their children because the schools—the public schools—were without question the best in the history of the world. I remember when I attended Mountain View Elementary School in Lynchburg, Virginia. I enrolled there in 1940 and spent six years there. Every week we attended chapel. Someone would read the Bible to all of the students and we would have prayer and sing hymns. We were taught to reverence God, the Bible, and prayer. Although, at that time, I was not a Christian and I did not know the Bible or have any religious knowledge, I gained a respect for God, the Bible, the church, and for things that were holy. I learned all those principles in a public school.

Until about thirty years ago, the public schools in America were providing that necessary support for our boys and girls. Christian education and the precepts of the Bible still permeated the curriculum of public schools. The Bible was read and prayer was of-

"...LET'S SEE NOW, YOU WANT SOMETHING WITHOUT VIOLENCE, SEX, SADISM, INTOLERANCE, UNCOUTH LANGUAGE, CRIME..."

fered in each and every school across our nation. But our public schools no longer teach Christian ethics, which educate children and young people intellectually, physically, emotionally, and spiritually. The Bible states, "The fear of the LORD is the beginning of knowledge." (Pr. 1:7) I believe that the decay in our public school system suffered an enormous acceleration when prayer and Bible reading were taken out of the classroom by the U.S. Supreme Court. Our public school system is now permeated with humanism. The human mind has been deceived, and the end result is that our schools are in serious trouble. . . .

Amoral Humanism

Humanism claims a "life adjustment" philosophy. The emphasis is placed on a person's social and psychological growth instead of on factual knowledge. "Socialization" has become the main purpose of education. Students are told that there are no absolutes and that they are to develop their own value systems. The humanist creed is documented in two humanist manifestos, signed in 1933 and 1973. Humanists believe that man is his own god and that moral values are relative, that ethics are situational. Humanists say that the Ten Commandments and other moral and ethical laws are "outmoded" and hindrances to human progress.

Humanism places man at the center of the universe. The philosophy of naturalism projects man as an animal concerned only with fulfilling the desires of the moment. It teaches that man is not a unique and specific creation of God. Man is merely the ultimate product of the evolutionary process who has gained a sense of intelligence that prevents him from acting like an animal.

Naturalism looks on man as a kind of biological machine. In that philosophy of life, sexual immorality is just another bodily function like eating or drinking. Man lives a meaningless existence in which the only important thing is for him to make himself happy in the here and now. It is a philosophy of "do your own thing." Its slogan is "If it feels good, do it." Neither philosophy offers moral absolutes, a right and a wrong. Not only are these philosophies destroying our educational system, but they are destroying the basis and the foundation of the Christian family as well.

Negating Basic Values

Basic values such as morality, individualism, respect for our nation's heritage, and the benefits of the free-enterprise system have, for the most part, been censored from today's public-classroom textbooks. From kindergarten right through the total school system, it almost seems as if classroom textbooks are designed to negate what philosophies previously had been taught. Under the guise of sex education or value clarification, many textbooks are actually perverting the minds of literally millions of students. Let me lay out a brief summary of quotes that I have taken from textbooks I have in hand. These textbooks are actually being used in the classrooms of our American schools. I have found quotes such as these: "To truly induce completely creative thinking we should teach children to question the Ten Commandments, patriotism, the two-party system, monogamy, and laws against incest."

Here is another: "It's tactless if not actually wrong not to lie under certain circumstances."

Another: "To be a better citizen a person needs to learn how to apply for welfare and how to burn the American flag."

"There are exceptions to almost all moral laws depending on the situation."

"Honesty is not something you either have or don't have."

"American society is ugly, trashy, cheap, and commercial, it is dehumanizing, its middle-class values are seen as arbitrary, materialistic, narrow, and hypocritical."

"To be successful in our culture one must learn to dream of failure."

"Only by remaining absurd can one feel free from fear."

A textbook entitled *Human Sexuality: A Course for Young Adults* was approved by the California State Board of Education. Recommended to the board by the State Commission on Curriculum, the book is intended for children aged twelve to fourteen, in the seventh and eighth grades. Sex is described explicitly in words and pictures. The book advises children that because parents are old-fashioned and narrow-minded about moral values, the home is the worst place to learn about sex. It presents the view that perversion is in the eyes of the beholder, saying that unusual sexual behavior should not be considered a perversion simply because it is out of the ordinary. Students are informed that strong disapproval of premarital sexual activity is not shared by the majority of the world's cultures. Infidelity is condoned. The book spoke about subjects such as homosexuality, incest, masochism, masturbation, sadism, and nymphomania.

Many parents would be appalled and shocked if they examined the textbooks from which their children are being taught in America's schools today. Books are very significant factors in society. The textbook business for elementary and secondary schools is an $823-million-a-year business.

Need for Censorship

Censorship has become a necessity because perverted educators have felt that presenting life in the raw produced a better product than the tried and proven methods of a few generations ago . . . with their emphasis on morality, integrity and striving for perfection.

Robert Billings, quoted in *Censorship News*, March 1982.

When you find an advanced society such as ours, you will find that books have played an important part in the development of that society. The Book of all books has been and always will be the Word of God, the Bible. The foundation for our government, our laws, our statutes, our civilization, the structures of our home, our states, and our churches have come from the Word of God. America's past greatness has come because she has honored the Bible. The attitude America's people take toward the Bible is in direct proportion to the stability of America as a nation. . . .

Anti-Value MACOS

Mel and Norma Gabler head a group called Educational Research Analysis. The Gablers have become known all across America for their efforts to improve the textbooks of America's schools. . . .

Mel Gabler points out in a pamphlet entitled *Have You Read Your Children's School Textbooks?* that the federal government has funded a particular series of studies called "MACOS," which stands for "Man: A Course of Study." Designed for fifth-grade children, this course was hailed by liberals when it came out in 1972 as one of the greatest programs ever developed. Supposedly, MACOS teaches why man is more human than other animals and so on. But as the Gablers have pointed out, the study includes wife-swapping, men practicing cannibalism, the killing of baby girls, and eleven-year-old students role-playing leaving their grandmothers to die. The thirty MACOS booklets are filled with more examples of such cruelty, violence, and death.

MACOS was produced by the National Science Foundation and was the brainchild of Jerome Bruner, a Harvard psychologist specializing in experimental behavior. MACOS was intended to teach the universal bond among all men through a series of discovery lessons on a variety of cultures. The aim was to have children step outside of their own cultures to question values that they may have already learned. The required training for teachers forbids any new questions or clarifications to be inserted. The teacher is helpless. All questions come from manuals that have to be followed exactly, and the students are not allowed to look for answers in extracurricular source material of their own or their parents. All answers must be obtained from the course books, the simulated games, and the films. MACOS is a perfect example of a closed system of government indoctrination for neutralizing the values taught by church and home.

Children who take this course are not to take their booklets home. When parents try to examine these booklets, they find it is very difficult. Parents should be prepared for such pacifying statements as, "The books teach realism; students should learn about other cultures." Students are faced with values that are anti-American, that equate man with the animals, and that display harsh attitudes toward a home and family. Children are taught that there are no absolute rights or absolute wrongs and that the traditional home is one alternative. Homosexuality is another. Decency is relative.

Inquiries in Sociology notes, "there are exceptions to almost all moral laws depending on the situation." (p. 37) But if God, or the integrity of the Bible, or creationism are included uncritically in a textbook, that book is immediately labeled as biased.

Indoctrinating Children

Hitler knew exactly how to indoctrinate people. He went right to the children and in their schoolrooms. Fascism was taught until at one point in time the children became his slaves. Children were ready and willing to turn their parents in to the state for disloyal statements. Prayer and Bible reading were taken out of the schools because they might "offend" some child who did not believe in God. The other 99 percent of the children had to listen to evolution and secularism, humanism, and vulgarity.

The textbook *Many Peoples, One Nation* (1973), contains this statement: "No nation on earth is guilty of practices more shocking and bloody than in the United States at this very hour." The National Education Association (NEA) is urging that a film, *The Unknown War*, put together by Soviet film makers, be shown to school children. The film is nothing less than Soviet propaganda.

In the book *Are Textbooks Harming Your Children?* author James Hefley points out that the Gablers were disturbed by a report from an NEA affiliate, the National Council for the Social Studies. The report, "The Study and Teaching of American History," helped to explain the changes in recent history texts. The report said: "Our principle for selecting what is basic in . . . history involves a reference to its predicted outcome. Our 'emphasis' will be determined by what we find going on in the present . . . Most of us have pledged our allegiance to an organized world community. . . . The teacher who adopts this principle of selection is as intellectually honest as the teacher who relies upon the textbook author—and far more creative. . . ." (p. 31) We find that public education has become materialistic, humanistic, atheistic, and socialistic. This is a far cry from what our Founding Fathers intended education to be. It is a far cry from the motto of the United States of America, "In God We Trust."

"It's my contention that some of those who are the most vocal in denouncing censorship today actually pose the greatest threat to free speech."

Radical Left Censorship Undermines Education

Cal Thomas

Cal Thomas, prize-winning conservative journalist and syndicated columnist, decries the hypocrisy of the left. In the following viewpoint, he says that liberals who accuse the religious right of censorship are guilty of the same thing but in a more underhanded way. Claiming to be broadening the minds of students by eliminating sexism, racism, ageism, and other "isms" from school materials, they are actually creating a false picture of reality, undermining traditional values, and preventing students from knowing the truth.

As you read, consider the following questions:

1. What does Mr. Thomas say is wrong with presenting a "balanced" view of the sexes?
2. In what sense does Mr. Thomas say that taxpayers are paying for the very propaganda that sabotages their values?
3. Does Mr. Thomas seem to believe that *only* majority values should be taught?

Today we hear a great deal about various threats to our First Amendment rights. It's my contention that some of those who are the most vocal in denouncing censorship today actually pose the greatest threat to free speech. Many of those with a purely secular vision of society, including some who exercised their right of free speech so forcefully in the past two decades, are slowly making a mockery of the First Amendment. The stench of their suppression of alternate viewpoints is no less offensive because they try to sweeten the foul odor with their own brand of "air freshener," appealing to "pluralism," "academic freedom," and "freedom of thought and expression.'

In reality these new secularist censors are as bad, and in many instances even worse, than the old censors because they attempt to prohibit ideas from reaching the shelves of libraries and bookstores and the pages of public school textbooks in the first place.

The modern censors don't show up at our doors with a book of matches, a can of gasoline, and a list of books that must be burned. Such a direct approach could be rather easily withstood. Neither do they plot together to these ends. But the subtle repression of alternate viewpoints to secularism occurs on a massive scale.

Modern Censors

The modern censors first manipulate and redefine language in a way that makes any challenge to their rule-setting appear intolerant and narrow-minded. Whatever they say, no matter how one-dimensional, no matter how blasphemous or scatalogical, must be treated with profound reverence. But God help anyone who utters the mildest protest or suggests that an alternative view should also be presented. Should such a person transgress and trespass on the holy ground of the mass media and academia, the full weight of their elitist condemnation will come crashing down around them like multi-targeted warheads. He or she will be dubbed (choose one or more, please) a censor, a bigot, an ayatollah, a fundamentalist, an underminer of the First Amendment, a religious fanatic, a Puritan, an ignoramus, or a book burner. . . . Our public schools have been entrusted with giving our children the general knowledge necessary to function well in society and the ability to explore further knowledge. Unfortunately, many people who shape our schools, from textbook writers to teachers, forget their position is a trust. They begin to see themselves, arrogantly, as the unchallengeable molders of future generations.

Indeed, the idea that the public schools ought to be used to educate children out of the "superstitious notions" their parents teach them and to convert them to the official ideology of the state has been around since the Enlightenment. It has also been used very effectively by totalitarian governments. And now that notion is cropping up ever more frequently in our own society.

The fact is, many of those who would supposedly make us more enlightened are actively undermining ideas that the majority in our society hold to be true. For example, regardless of their religious affiliations, most Americans still believe that boys and girls are different. Not only do they look different, but they also act in different ways. This makes romantic relationships complicated and interesting. Christians may base their claim that the sexes are different—and equally worthy—on their belief in Creation, but common sense leads to the same conclusion. According to a Gallup poll published in *Families* in June of 1982, 75 percent of all women still think the ideal way of living is to be married and have children. Yet textbooks are constantly eroding those ideas.

Self-Righteous "Protection"

Many feminists appear to think it is censorship when the Moral Majority attempts to suppress a book or magazine but good politics when the same thing is done in the name of feminism. Feminist book banning is characterized by hypocrisy and a self-serving double standard. When the Nazis burned books, they were just as self-righteous as feminist vigilantes. After all, they felt they were protecting women and children (from the alleged effects of "Jewish Bolshevism" and "degenerate" sexuality). When good twentieth-century feminists shoot out the windows of porn shops, call down the police on porn theatres, suppress the work of feminists with whom they do not agree, and agitate against the free exchange of ideas, they too think they are justified to "protect" women and children. They never consider themselves fascists.

Gayle Rubin, *Gay Community News*, December 22, 1984.

Michael Levin, a professor of philosophy at City College of New York, writes in an article in *Commentary* magazine that "one of the most extensive thought-control campaigns in American education history has gone completely ignored. I am referring to the transformation, in the name of 'sex fairness,' of textbooks and curricula at all educational levels, with the aim of convincing children that boys and girls are the same."

The major textbook publishers—such as McGraw-Hill, Macmillan, Harper & Row, Lippincott, Rand McNally, Silver Burdett, Scott-Foresman, Laidlaw Brothers, and South-Western— have lists of guidelines requiring their writers to promote a feminist world view, according to Levin. . . . The result of these guidelines, according to Levin, is "a basic incoherence of purpose, between showing the world as it is and as ideological feminists believe it ought to be." . . .

160

Publishers are painfully meticulous about presenting a "balanced" view of the sexes in the material represented, in text and illustrations. "The treatment of science is especially tortured," Levin says of one publisher's books, "since Macmillan cannot quite bring itself to admit that most scientific discoveries were actually made by men." The publisher's solution is to say that "white males are credited with" most scientific achievements. "For all the pretense of balance, however, the one activity never depicted favorably in these guidelines is motherhood," Levin adds.

Confusing Children

As a result of cumulative brainwashing, he says, children must be extremely confused by the difference between what they *read* about sex roles and what they actually *see* in their own homes and neighborhoods. (Most school children do have mothers, for example, many of whom are full-time mothers at that, or secretaries instead of truck drivers. A great many school children also have fathers, some of whom are doctors, or work at garages instead of day care centers.) According to the Bureau of Labor statistics, 13,323,000 women, or 41.5 percent of those with children under age eighteen, are not in the labor force. But you wouldn't know it from reading the feminist-influenced textbooks. If children recognize the distortion between what they see and read, they may develop "scorn for the mendacity of their elders," according to Levin.

In my judgment, an even more dangerous prospect is that second graders may *not* be able to articulate discrepancies between the real and the "ideal," but will absorb the feminist propaganda in their readers. Then they will scorn not the textbooks for lying, but their parents for not following feminist prescriptions. . . .

Federally Assisted Censorship

An important and disturbing element of the feminist textbook issue is that many projects designed to make our children sex-blind or disdainful of the family structure receive assistance from the federal government. In other words, *we* are paying for the propaganda. This is censorship in the strict sense; control of information by governmental authority. . . .

The Council on Interracial Books for Children, which receives funds from the federal government, takes an activist approach to "sexism," "ageism," "classism," "handicapism" and other such "isms" and also warns against giving children illusions about democracy:

Implicit in all of the textbooks surveyed is the assumption that U.S. society is a true democracy, by virtue of its electoral system in which citizens can vote for the leader of their choice. . . . Furthermore, it is assumed that a democratic government like ours is the best of all possible governments. Perhaps it really is best, but the textbooks describe "communist" and "socialist" nations by their economic systems, while rarely describing U.S. society in terms of its capitalist economic system. This muddies comparisons of both economies and governments. The distortion which results is serious, for by calling both our governments and economic system "democratic," the textbooks deny the realities of capitalism and all that goes with it—classes, conflicting class interests, and the ongoing struggle between those few who control wealth and those many who are trying to share the wealth.

It is right to expose school children to the weaknesses of our country and encourage them to improve society, but the Council seems to advocate turning our tax-supported public schools into socialist, utopian guerrilla training camps. In promoting the "truly feminist vision," they are trying to create a sexless, family-less utopia. And yet we never hear of these people as "censors." They are "bettering society." Nonsense. The cumulative effect of such blatant efforts to rewrite history and revolutionize accepted mores is not only to censor out any trace of Christian values, but to eradicate any values at all, save those of the people doing the censoring.

"Some of the most influential anti-censorship forces have done a great disservice to those who seek race and sex equality in the schools."

The Left Must Guard American Values

Fred L. Pincus

While most censorship criticism is leveled at the religious right, liberals are receiving more attention in this respect. Critics point out that removing a book from a library because it portrays women in a stereotypical manner is just as much an act of censorship as removing a book because it presents a Communist view. Fred L. Pincus, an assistant professor of sociology at the University of Maryland, Baltimore County, is the education writer for the liberal news weekly *The Guardian*. He resents having efforts to remove sexism, racism, and other "isms" from school materials labeled "censorship." These efforts are essential, he writes in the following viewpoint, if society's attitudes are to be changed.

As you read, consider the following questions:

1. Why does Mr. Pincus believe it is unfair to compare removal of racial stereotypes to removal of descriptions of sex and drug use?
2. According to Mr. Pincus, such groups as the Council on Interracial Books for Children do not want to *censor*. What *do* they want to do?

Fred L. Pincus, "Censorship in the Name of Civil Rights: A View from the Left," *Education Week*, January 26, 1983. Reprinted by permission.

Many individuals and groups who have opposed censorship in the public schools have made an important contribution in the fight to oppose the growing strength of the New Right. At the same time, some of the most influential anti-censorship forces have done a great disservice to those who seek race and sex equality in the schools.

People like Nat Hentoff (*Village Voice* columnist and author of *The First Freedom*), Judith Krug (head of the American Library Association's Office for Intellectual Freedom), Edward P. Jenkinson (chairman of the National Council of Teachers of English's (N.C.T.E.) Committee Against Censorship), and Lee Burress (incoming chairman of the N.C.T.E. committee) spend a disproportionate amount of time criticizing feminist and anti-racist groups that are trying to improve the images of women and minorities in schoolbooks—so-called "censors of the Left."

Insulating Schools

The goal of Mr. Hentoff and the others is to insulate the schools from *any* external pressures, whether they are applied from the Right or the Left. They argue that parental input that goes beyond explicit support of current school policy is potentially dangerous. While most of the anti-censorship groups view censors of the Left as a secondary problem to right-wing groups, Mr. Hentoff, on the other hand, recently went so far as to say, "I'm less worried about the fundamentalists than [about] these seemingly benign folks who want to protect children. They don't want sexist books near a child." He also expressed concern about the "nice" people who objected to racist books.

Such reasoning leads to the outrageous conclusion that objecting to racial stereotypes in *Little Black Sambo* or to sex-role stereotypes found in most children's readers is as bad as objecting to the frank discussion of drugs and sex in *Go Ask Alice*, or to a critical discussion of U.S. policy toward minorities in a history textbook. After all, the argument goes, censorship is censorship.

Clearly, this attitude helps to retard the development of nonracist and nonsexist curricula. But it also alienates feminist and anti-racist groups that are actually potential allies in the fight against the New Right. And it provides more ammunition for members of the New Right to use in their attempts to turn back the educational clock.

Left "Censors" Are Correct

But unfortunately for Mr. Hentoff and his colleagues, the empirical evidence shows that, by and large, the "Left censors" are correct in their criticisms of the schools. Empirical studies have shown that prior to 1970, schoolbooks either treated women and minorities in stereotyped ways or ignored them altogether. And although there was some progress during the 1970's, the basic problem still exists.

A 1980 U.S. Commission on Civil Rights Report, *Characters in Textbooks*, concludes that during the past decade, "blacks were still stereotyped in certain occupational roles, primarily service work, sports, and entertainment. There was a strong tendency to present romanticized versions of black life and to avoid or deny the actual conditions in which many blacks have existed. . . . Women and girls were typically featured in stories with themes of dependency and domesticity. They also appeared in relatively few jobs outside the home."

Actually, most of the feminist and anti-racist groups like the Council on Interracial Books for Children, the National Organization for Women, and the National Association for the Advancement of Colored People are not primarily interested in censorship. They want books to *expand* the treatment of women and minorities. When they find books in use in the schools that fall short of this goal, these groups are usually able to recommend alternatives that are more comprehensive and more sensitive to these issues.

Respect for Diversity

Publishers recognize that textbooks carry a social as well as an educational message. The publishing industry supports the belief that the acceptance of human diversity is a fundamental American value and maintains that through exposure to such diversity children develop a sense of respect for themselves and for people of different backgrounds.

Textbook Publishers and the Censorship Controversy, Association of American Publishers, 1981.

It is obvious that the New Right objects to the goals of feminist and anti-racist groups. Is it also true that some liberals who oppose censorship also oppose racial and sexual equality in school books? It seems, at least, that the actions of Mr. Hentoff and his liberal colleagues help to preserve the not-very-equitable status quo.

Censorship vs. Guidelines

Their argument also leaves little room for parents to participate in the educational process of their children. The N.C.T.E. board of directors, for example, recently differentiated between "censoring textbooks and other teaching materials and setting guidelines for selection of such materials. . . . Whereas censors are motivated by content they find objectionable, guideline writers are motivated by content that the professionally trained find educationally sound and effective."

165

This sounds very nice, but what are parents to do when they find that many racist and sexist books have been called "educationally sound" by the "professionally trained"? Neither educators nor book publishers have an unblemished record when it comes to being free from stereotypes. Unfortunately, it is still necessary for parents and feminist and anti-racist groups to educate the educators and the publishers. Questioning the use of certain books may sometimes be an essential part of that process.

Ironically, taking the position that "only the educators can decide" actually strengthens the position of the New Right. The Moral Majority and other right-wing groups tell parents that educators are elitist and afraid of the public. Mel and Norma Gabler, the most influential of the New Right "textbook analysts" tell parents: "To educators, you are an 'outsider' who is 'infringing' in 'their' arena when you question or even examine school subject matter."

The New Right calls on parents to organize in order to rid the schools of "anti-Christian" and "anti-American" books. This, in turn, is supposed to increase the effectiveness of the nation's schools.

This simplistic populist rhetoric is used to manipulate parents who are frustrated by complex problems in the schools and in the larger society. Rather than proposing just and realistic solutions, the New Right's educational policies promote white supremacy, male domination, religious ethnocentrism, and knee-jerk patriotism.

Virtually all recent studies show that censorship attempts by organized New Right groups are on the increase. This dangerous trend cannot be stopped by trying to insulate the schools from outside contact.

Honestly Evaluate Criticism

Educators should not wrap themselves in the mantle of moderation to protect themselves from "extremists of the Left." Rather, they should reach out to parents and feminist and anti-racist groups by encouraging and honestly evaluating their criticisms and suggestions.

166

"When we act to suppress what we do not like, we . . . . deny and reject the very essence of Americanism."

All Censorship Is Un-American

David K. Berninghausen

David K. Berninghausen is a professor of library science at the University of Minnesota in Minneapolis. It is his contention that dangerous censorship impulses come from both the left and the right and that both are equally threatening to the American concept of free debate of ideas. In the following viewpoint, he states that it is common to all people to *want* to censor certain ideas that are abhorrent to them. But it is when people *act* on their inclinations that freedom becomes endangered.

As you read, consider the following questions:

1. What are some examples cited by the author showing censorship attempts by the religious right? by the liberal left?
2. For what reason, according to the author, do organizations and individuals *want* to censor?
3. What does Mr. Berninghausen say is "the essence of Americanism"?
4. According to the author, why does the fact that society is "in trouble" not justify censorship?

David K. Berninghausen, "The Arrogance of the Censor," reprinted from *USA Today*, March 1982. Copyright 1982 by The Society for the Advancement of Education.

Pressures upon schools and libraries to ban what partisans dislike come from both the extreme left and the extreme right. What is common to all censors is that they utterly reject a pluralistic society and its major premises. In Eric Sevareid's words, they are filled with "dangerously passionate certainties." They arrogate to themselves the right to impose those "passionate certainties" on everyone. It is a short step from that position for them to feel justified in censoring materials with which they do not agree or, perhaps, with expressions which they do not understand.

Possibly, the censors find it inconceivable that a librarian or teacher could hold up for examination expressions of various points of view impartially, encouraging citizens and students to weigh the evidence supporting or refuting a proposition. They do, in fact, feel that schools ought not to teach children to critically examine issues, that to do so is to promote atheism, since truth is already known.

It is certain that, by their behavior of suppressing what they do not like, censors manifest their rejection of Judge Learned Hand's thought that "truth is more likely to be gathered from a multitude of tongues than through any kind of authoritative selection."

Truth Through Pluralism

One of America's wisest and most articulate judges, Learned Hand has noted that many human beings, both in America and elsewhere, are unwilling or unready to accept the theory of free expression and free inquiry as it has been developed in American society. As is true with olives or scotch whiskey, a taste for intellectual freedom is one which must be acquired, and some who learn to like it for themselves try vigorously to deny it to others. During the 1970's, this was expressed by New Left students on campuses from coast to coast with their battle cry: "We demand free speech and you shut up!"

Judge Hand observed that, although many people consider it utterly foolish, America has bet its life on the theory expressed in the First Amendment to the Constitution:

> Congress shall make no law respecting an establishment of religion, or prohibiting the free exercise thereof; or abridging the freedom of speech, or of the press, or the right of the people peaceably to assemble, and to petition the Government for a redress of grievances.

From this freedom, which Supreme Court Justice Benjamin Cardozo called the cornerstone of a free society, flow all other freedoms. Yet, in the last decade, as special-interest and single-issue groups have developed, they have subordinated the principle of free speech, press, and inquiry to some other cause which they view as holding a priority over every other principle. The primacy of the First Amendment is thus denied.

For example, the segment of society called the Moral Majority apparently places intellectual freedom for individuals far below anti-evolution, anti-abortion, anti-homosexualism, or prayer in the schools. Similarly, when ethnic groups attempt to purge libraries of what they perceive as sexist, racist, or individualist materials, they also subordinate free expression and inquiry to their special causes.

No Right to Impose Values

No group has the right to impose its own ideas of politics, morality or religion upon other members of a democratic society. Freedom does not exist if it is given only to the accepted and inoffensive.

From a statement by residents, Niles, Michigan, quoted in *Censorship News*, January 1983.

Censors seem unable to understand the significance of a pluralistic American society. They cannot tolerate free expression. They reject the theory of a "multitude of tongues," insisting that everyone must believe in and follow their single moral philosophy. Whether their target is what they view as obscene, blasphemous, sexist, racist, subversive, or something else which is offensive in their perception, censors try to use public opinion and government to control what people read, see, and hear. This kind of coercion is well-illustrated by the behavior and tactics of the Moral Majority.

Appeal to Fear of Change

The common thread is an appeal to fear of change. Through the fund-raising efforts of the New Right, substantial sums are used to buy media time and to produce literature which uses propaganda techniques to discredit "liberal" teachers, librarians, and institutions. Prejudicial labeling, using such words as "anti-family," "anti-God," and "secular humanism," is one technique. Quotations taken out of context is another. Overgeneralization, arguing from one isolated example, is common. Sometimes, teachers or librarians are harassed by phone calls in the middle of the night and threatened. In West Virginia, schools were bombed following polarization over curriculum materials. In this case, church groups were urged to violence by fundamentalist preachers and agitators from outside the state. . . .

Most librarians support the theory of the First Amendment, that men can live well together if they, as individuals, have access to expressions of all points of view, freedom to hear and see and examine all propositions, finally forming their own personal judgment as to which are sound and valid. In order to get the truth, conflicting arguments and expressions must be allowed. There can be no freedom without choice, no sound choice without knowledge.

This American theory of intellectual freedom demands that discussion must be kept open, that no assumption or opinion can be excepted. It is regarded as an essential condition for the operation of a democratic society that, if a citizen is to have an opportunity to choose between rival propositions and courses of action, he must know what they are; hence, he may not be denied the opportunity to hear and read about them.

Almost every American finds that there are some subjects upon which his tolerance threshold is very low. Frequently, we may be tempted to say: "Of course I am against censorship, but, on *this* topic, at this time, for this audience, we must make an exception and prohibit full, free access to all points of view."

Action, Not Temptation Is Censorship

When we *act* to suppress what we do not like, we give evidence that we are suffering from an attack of arrogance. We are asserting that we *know* with absolute certainty, that our own beliefs and values are correct and moral, and that any contrary expression is immoral and must be banned. We deny the rights of all others to hold opinions contrary to ours and to express them. We thus deny and reject the very essence of Americanism—that we cherish the opportunity to live in a pluralistic society, where every citizen has equal rights to inform himself on all subjects and exercise his powers of reason.

Censors characteristically deny both the primacy and the indivisibility of the principle of free expression. They argue that certain issues are "undebatable"; hence, censorship of expressions which may do harm is necessary. Their view of the nature of a library fits the authoritarian mold, rather than the democratic. The censor of libraries argues that the presence of a book or film which he perceives as "bad" proves that the librarian and the library endorse and promote what to him is abhorrent. The censor then demands that what he does not like shall be removed. . . .

We live in demanding times. The list of organizations and individuals who arrogate to themselves the power to control what others shall read, see, hear, or study is almost unlimited. Their demands are heard everywhere. They say: "We speak for 'the people.'" "Anyone who is not with us is against us." "We demand free speech for ourselves, but not for you."

In January, 1980, at a First Amendment Congress in Philadelphia, a Gallup poll reported that three out of four U.S. citizens could not name the provisions of the First Amendment; that six out of ten with a college background were unable to answer such questions. If this was an accurate survey, then the guarantees of the First Amendment can not be counted on to endure. The rights to free speech, a free press, free choice of religion, and free assembly are not very secure.

Freedom Is American Privilege and Responsibility

In a larger frame of reference, we note that the United Nations Declaration of Universal Human Rights emphasizes the significance of free speech and free press. Less than 20% of the 4,500,000,000 human beings on our planet have experienced even a small degree of free access to all points of view on all issues. More than 80% have been denied the opportunity to form their own informed, personal judgments. In contrast to most of the people on Earth, Americans *may* express dissent with government decisions, but, if they honor the First Amendment, they *may not* suppress the views of others.

Lack of Trust

Censorship, in any form, represents a lack of trust in the judgment and discrimination of the individual. The passage of time provides the best perspective for sorting the wheat from the chaff.

Bruce E. Fleury, *Christian Science Monitor*, November 19, 1982.

Today, there are many signs that our society is in trouble. This is nothing new. All societies are always in trouble. However, as long as the First Amendment is in effect, as long as individual citizens have the opportunity to examine all the evidence and to make informed judgments, there is a chance that we will find ways of resolving our problems.

The censor, right or left, would take away this chance. When the censor wins, everybody loses.

Understanding Words in Context

Readers occasionally come across words which they do not recognize. And frequently, because they do not know a word or words, they will not fully understand the passage being read. Obviously, the reader can look up an unfamiliar word in a dictionary. However, by carefully examining the word in the context in which it is used, the word's meaning can often be determined. A careful reader may find clues to the meaning of the word in surrounding words, ideas, and attitudes.

Below are excerpts from the viewpoints in this chapter. In each excerpt, one or two words are printed in italics. Try to determine the meaning of each word by reading the excerpt. Under each excerpt you will find four definitions for the italicized word. Choose the one that is closest to your understanding of the word.

Finally, use a dictionary to see how well you have understood the words in context. It will be helpful to discuss with others the clues which helped you decide on each word's meaning.

1. Books are burned and banned because of the philosophy the right finds particularly *NOXIOUS*.

   NOXIOUS means:
   a) interesting   c) correct
   b) smelly   d) bad

2. It's my *CONTENTION* that some of those who are the most vocal in denouncing censorship today actually pose the greatest threat to free speech.

   CONTENTION means:
   a) argument   c) pleasure
   b) disagreement   d) relief

3. The *STENCH* of their suppression of alternate viewpoints is no less offensive because they try to sweeten the foul odor with their own brand of "air freshener."

   STENCH means:
   a) complaint   c) stink
   b) cause   d) rightness

4. They begin to see themselves, *ARROGANTLY*, as the un-challengeable molders of future generations.

ARROGANTLY means:
a) stupidly
b) conceitedly
c) oddly
d) wisely

5. Publishers are painfully *METICULOUS* about presenting a "balanced" view of the sexes in the material represented, but one activity never depicted favorably is motherhood.

METICULOUS means:
a) inadequate
b) balanced
c) unbalanced
d) careful

6. The effect of such efforts to rewrite history and revolutionize accepted values is not only to censor out any trace of Christian values, but to *ERADICATE* any values at all, save those of the people doing the censoring.

ERADICATE means:
a) emphasize
b) wipe out
c) censor
d) distort

7. They *ARROGATE TO* themselves the right to impose their beliefs on everyone.

ARROGATE TO means:
a) take over for
b) remove from
c) add water to
d) destroy for

8. Possibly, the censors find it inconceivable that a librarian or teacher could hold up for examination expressions of various points of view impartially, encouraging citizens and students to weigh the evidence supporting or *REFUTING* a proposition.

REFUTING means:
a) supporting
b) explaining
c) disagreeing with
d) describing

9. Censors seem unable to understand the significance of a *PLURALISTIC* American society. They reject the theory of a "multitude of tongues," insisting that everyone must believe in and follow their single moral theory.

PLURALISTIC means:
a) having multiple characteristics
b) isolated
c) unified
d) shattered

Periodical Bibliography

The following list of periodical articles deals with the subject matter of this chapter.

Margot Allen
"Huck Finn: Two Generations of Pain," *Interracial Books for Children Bulletin*, Volume 15, Number 5, 1984.

Teresa Carpenter
"Book Banners," *Redbook*, January 1983.

Frances Fitzgerald
"A Reporter at Large: Disagreement in Baileyville," *The New Yorker*, January 16, 1984.

Barbara J. Hampton
"Sense & Censorship," *Eternity*, September 1983.

Patricia Hancock
"In the Shadow of Guidelines," *Social Studies Teacher*, April-June 1985.

James Hefley and Harold Smith
"What Should Johnny Read," *Christianity Today*, September 7, 1984.

Nat Hentoff
"The Dumbing of America," *The Progressive*, February 1984.

M.M. Kambi
"Censorship vs. Selection—Choosing Books for Schools," *American Education*, March 1982.

Michael Levin
"Feminism & Thought Control," *Commentary*, June 1982.

Onalee McGraw
"Censorship and the Public Schools: Who Decides What Students Will Read?" *American Education*, December 1982.

The Phyllis Schlafly Report
Issue on censorship, February 1983. Available from Box 618, Alton, IL 62002.

USA Today
Forum on censorship, Opinion Page, November 16, 1984.

Judi Lawson Wallace
"What Kids Read—Who Decides?" *Ms.*, April 1985.

Elsa Walsh
"Taking Real Life Out of Textbooks," *The Washington Post National Weekly Edition*, December 3, 1984.

Dorothy Wickenden
"Bowdlerizing The Bard," *The New Republic*, June 3, 1985.

George F. Will
"Huck at a Hundred," *Newsweek*, February 18, 1985.

Should Pornography Be Censored?

Chapter Preface

The problem of pornography has long been debated by civil libertarians, conservatives, feminists, and the general public. While there is a small faction which believes that pornography is not only harmless but may even be beneficial, more people believe that it is damaging to individuals and society. However, there is little agreement on what to do about it.

Traditionally, the answers to the problems of regulating pornography have been divided along political lines: Liberals said it was repulsive but that it was protected by the First Amendment. Conservatives said that it was repulsive and harmful and therefore was *not* protected by the First Amendment.

In 1983, however, a new approach was taken which united conservatives and many traditionally liberal feminists against liberals and other feminists. The City Council of Minneapolis, Minnesota, distressed by the growing impact of pornography, determined to do something about it. They commissioned two feminists with legal and aesthetic anti-pornography experience to draft a law that would eliminate the old confusions about definitions.

The authors' approach was a unique one: Instead of looking at the subject as a free speech issue revolving around the civil rights of pornographers, they chose to protect the civil rights of the people they perceived as the *victims* of pornography—primarily women and children.

The law they drafted was extremely controversial. Its constitutionality was widely debated. Despite the Minneapolis mayor's veto, the impact of the proposition was nation-wide. Shortly after the Minneapolis debates, similar laws underwent lively debates in Indianapolis, New York, Los Angeles, and several other communities. While the nation still awaits a higher court ruling on the constitutionality of the "Minneapolis ordinance," it has offered a new tactic to those who wish to control pornography.

176

> *"Pornography is a systematic practice of exploitation and subordination based on sex that differentially harms women."*

Pornography Violates Women's Civil Rights

Andrea Dworkin and Catharine MacKinnon

The following viewpoint, a model antipornography law drafted by Andrea Dworkin and Catharine MacKinnon, defines pornography and explains how it is a violation of civil rights. Ms. Dworkin is a feminist author who has written extensively on pornography. Her 1981 book *Pornography: Men Possessing Women* graphically describes her perceptions of pornography as a patriarchal institution which keeps women in a position of inferiority. Ms. MacKinnon, a feminist and a professor of law, has worked actively to change pornography laws around the nation.

As you read, consider the following questions:

1. In what ways, according to this viewpoint, does pornography harm people?
2. One problem with previous antipornography laws is that their definitions have been too vague. Judges and juries have had a difficult time determining if an item should legally be considered pornography. Does it look to you as if that would still be a problem with this law? Why or why not?

Andrea Dworkin and Catharine MacKinnon, "Model Antipornography Law," *Ms.*, April 1985. Reprinted with permission.

The following model civil rights law differs somewhat from earlier versions originally introduced in Minneapolis and Indianapolis.

Section 1. Statement of Policy

Pornography is sex discrimination. It exists in [PLACE], posing a substantial threat to the health, safety, peace, welfare, and equality of citizens in the community. Existing [state and] federal laws are inadequate to solve these problems in [PLACE].

Pornography is a systematic practice of exploitation and subordination based on sex that differentially harms women. The harm of pornography includes dehumanization, sexual exploitation, forced sex, forced prostitution, physical injury, and social and sexual terrorism and inferiority presented as entertainment. The bigotry and contempt it promotes, with the acts of aggression it fosters, diminish opportunities for equality of rights in employment, education, property, public accommodations and public services; create public and private harassment, persecution and denigration; promote injury and degradation such as rape, battery, child sexual abuse, and prostitution and inhibit just enforcement of laws against these acts; contribute significantly to restricting women in particular from full exercise of citizenship and participation in public life, including in neighborhoods; damage relations between the sexes; and undermine women's equal exercise of rights to speech and action guaranteed to all citizens under the Constitutions and laws of the United States and [PLACE, INCLUDING STATE].

Section 2. Definitions

1. *Pornography* is the graphic sexually explicit subordination of women through pictures and/or words that also includes one or more of the following: (i) women are presented dehumanized as sexual objects, things, or commodities; or (ii) women are presented as sexual objects who enjoy pain or humiliation; or (iii) women are presented as sexual objects who experience sexual pleasure in being raped; or (iv) women are presented as sexual objects tied up or cut up or mutilated or bruised or physically hurt; or (v) women are presented in postures or positions of sexual submission, servility, or display; or (vi) women's body parts—including but not limited to vaginas, breasts, or buttocks—are exhibited such that women are reduced to those parts; or (vii) women are presented as whores by nature; or (viii) women are presented being penetrated by objects or animals; or (ix) women are presented in scenarios of degradation, injury, torture, shown as filthy or inferior, bleeding, bruised, or hurt in a context that makes these conditions sexual.

2. The use of men, children, or transsexuals in the place of women in (1) above is pornography for purposes of this law.

178

Section 3. Unlawful Practices

1. *Coercion into pornography:* It shall be sex discrimination to coerce, intimidate, or fraudulently induce (hereafter, "coerce") any person, including transsexual, into performing for pornography, which injury may date from any appearance or sale of any product(s) of such performance(s). The maker(s), seller(s), exhibitor(s), and/or distributor(s) of said pornography may be sued for damages and for an injunction, including to eliminate the product(s) of the performance(s) from the public view.

Porn Degrades

Pornography is *anti-woman.* The outright degradation and humiliation of women are the central themes of pornographic stories and pictures. In soft pornography, the victimization is less obvious but nonetheless present, as women are treated as sex-objects, disposable creatures to be ogled, used and abused, and then discarded in favor of another.

John H. Court, *Pornography: A Christian Critique,* 1980.

Proof of one or more of the following facts or conditions shall not, without more, negate a finding of coercion: (i) that the person is a woman; or (ii) that the person is or has been a prostitute; or (iii) that the person has attained the age of majority; or (iv) that the person is connected by blood or marriage to anyone involved in or related to the making of the pornography; or (v) that the person has previously had, or been thought to have had, sexual relations with anyone, including anyone involved in or related to the making of the pornography; or (vi) that the person has previously posed for sexually explicit pictures with or for anyone, including anyone involved in or related to the making of the pornography at issue; or (vii) that anyone else, including a spouse or other relative, has given permission on the person's behalf; or (viii) that the person actually consented to a use of the performance that is changed into pornography; or (ix) that the person knew that the purpose of the acts or events in question was to make pornography; or (x) that the person showed no resistance or appeared to cooperate actively in the photographic sessions or in the events that produced the pornography; or (xi) that the person signed a contract, or made statements affirming a willingness to cooperate in the production of pornography; or (xii) that no physical force, threats, or weapons were used in the making of the pornography; or (xiii) that the person was paid or otherwise compensated.

2. *Trafficking in pornography:* It shall be sex discrimination to produce, sell, exhibit, or distribute pornography, including through private clubs.

(i) City, state, and federally funded public libraries or private and public university and college libraries in which pornography is available for study, including on open shelves but excluding special display presentations, shall not be construed to be trafficking in pornography.

(ii) Isolated passages or isolated parts shall not be actionable under this section.

(iii) Any woman has a claim hereunder as a woman acting against the subordination of women. Any man, child, or transsexual who alleges injury by pornography in the way women are injured by it also has a claim.

3. *Forcing pornography on a person:* It shall be sex discrimination to force pornography on a person, including child or transsexual, in any place of employment, education, home, or public place. Only the perpetrator of the force or responsible institution may be sued.

4. *Assault or physical attack due to pornography:* It shall be sex discrimination to assault, physically attack, or injure any person, including child or transsexual, in a way that is directly caused by specific pornography. The perpetrator of the assault or attack may be sued for damages and enjoined where appropriate. The maker(s), distributor(s), seller(s), and/or exhibitor(s) may also be sued for damages and for an injunction against the specific pornography's further exhibition, distribution, or sale.

Section 4. Defenses

1. It shall not be a defense that the defendant in an action under this law did not know or intend that the materials were pornography or sex discrimination.

2. No damages or compensation for losses shall be recoverable under Sec. 3(2) or other than against the perpetrator of the assault or attack in Sec. 3(4) unless the defendant knew or had reason to know that the materials were pornography.

3. In actions under Sec. 3(2) or other than against the perpetrator of the assault or attack in Sec. 3(4), no damages or compensation for losses shall be recoverable against maker(s) for pornography made, against distributor(s) for pornography distributed, against seller(s) for pornography sold, or against exhibitor(s) for pornography exhibited, prior to the effective date of this law.

Section 5. Enforcement

In the event that this law is amended to a preexisting human-rights law, the complaint would first be made to a Civil Rights Commission. Any injunction issued under Sec. 3(2), the trafficking provision, would require trial *do novo* (a full court trial after the administrative hearing).

1. *Civil action:* Any person aggrieved by violations of this law may enforce its provisions by means of a civil action. No criminal penalties shall attach for any violation of the provisions of this law. Relief for violation of this act may include reasonable attorney's fees.

2. *Injunction:* Any person who violates this law may be enjoined except that:

(i) In actions under Sec. 3(2), and other than against the perpetrator of the assault or attack under Sec. 3(4), no temporary or permanent injunction shall issue prior to a final judicial determination that the challenged activities constitute a violation of this law.

(ii) No temporary or permanent injunction shall extend beyond such material(s) that, having been described with reasonable specificity by the injunction, have been determined to be validly proscribed under this law.

Section 6. Severability

Should any part(s) of this law be found legally invalid, the remaining part(s) remains valid. A judicial declaration that any part(s) of this law cannot be applied validly in a particular manner or to a particular case or category of cases shall not affect the validity of that part(s) as otherwise applied, unless such other application would clearly frustrate the [LEGISLATIVE BODY'S] intent in adopting this law.

Section 7. Limitation of Action

Actions under this law must be filed within one year of the alleged discriminatory acts.

"An attempt to deal with the problem of pornography through governmental suppression would involve a dangerous emasculation of the First Amendment."

Censoring Pornography Would Violate Civil Rights

Thomas I. Emerson

Thomas I. Emerson, a professor at Yale's School of Law, holds that there is no justification for inhibiting free speech in the case of pornography. In the following viewpoint, he responds specifically to the Minneapolis Ordinance, the prototype of the civil rights anti-pornography laws exemplified by the first viewpoint in this chapter.

As you read, consider the following questions:

1. Professor Emerson states that the government is not free to achieve desirable goals by suppressing certain forms of expression. Does he recommend other methods to achieve the same goals?
2. For what reasons, besides violating the first amendment, would banning pornography be bad, according to Professor Emerson?

Thomas I. Emerson, "Pornography and the First Amendment: A Reply to Professor MacKinnon," unpublished paper, April 16, 1984. Reprinted with the author's permission.

My concern arises not from Professor MacKinnon's statement of the problem of pornography but from her proposals for a solution. Despite her opening remark that "pornography cannot be reformed or suppressed or banned," but "can only be changed," it is clear that Professor MacKinnon would deal with the problem by invoking the power of the government to suppress pornography. Her specific proposals are embodied in the Minneapolis Ordinance, which she and Ms. Andrea Dworkin drafted. . . .

The sweep of the Minneapolis Ordinance is breathtaking. It would subject to governmental ban virtually all depictions of rape, verbal or pictorial, and indeed most presentations of sexual encounters. More specifically, it would outlaw such works of literature as D. H. Lawrence's *Lady Chatterly's Lover,* Henry Miller's *Tropic of Cancer,* William Faulkner's *Sanctuary,* Ernest Hemingway's *For Whom the Bell Tolls,* and Norman Mailer's *Advertisements for Myself,* to name but a few. The ban would indeed extend as far as Shakespeare, and perhaps to the Bible, in one direction and to the millions of copies of the "romance novels" now being sold in the super-markets in the other. It would embrace much of the world's art, from ancient carvings to Picasso, well-known films too numerous to mention, and a substantial part of commercial advertising. . . .

No Constitutional Support

If we test Professor MacKinnon's proposals against traditional First Amendment doctrine there is no way that her solution of the pornographic problem can be sustained . . . . The core element in First Amendment theory is that the impact of speech, whether considered good, bad or indifferent, cannot be invoked as a basis for government control of speech. Speech, or more generally expression, occupies a specially protected place in a democratic society. As a general proposition it cannot be prohibited, curtailed or interferred with by government authorities; the state must seek to achieve its social goals by methods other than the suppression of expression. This is the bedrock of the First Amendment. Were it otherwise the government could outlaw or regulate expression that hampered the effectiveness of government operations, urged basic reform in our society, opposed government policies abroad, or cast aspersions on fellow citizens. Clearly the suppression of pornographic speech, on the ground that it causes or reflects discrimination against women, would run afoul of this basic mandate of the First Amendment.

The Supreme Court has, of course, made some exceptions to the constitutional protection afforded freedom of expression. But it has never countenanced any degree of control that would create the gaping hole in our system of freedom of expression that the attempted suppression of "pornography" would open.

The exception that bears the closest resemblance to proposals for an official ban on pornography is found in the law concerning obscenity. In its obscenity decisions the Supreme Court has ruled that the government may prohibit the dissemination of materials "which taken as whole, appeal to the prurient interest in sex, which portray sexual conduct in a patently offensive way, and which, taken as a whole, do not have serious literary, artistic, political, or scientific value." The theory upon which the Supreme Court permits the suppression on obscenity, as thus defined, is the legal fiction that "obscenity is not within the area of constitutionally protected speech," in other words that obscenity is not covered by the First Amendment at all. It is inconceivable, however, that the Supreme Court would hold that the far broader area of "pornography" is simply outside the scope of First Amendment protections. More importantly, as Professor MacKinnon points out, the social goals sought by the

obscenity laws are essentially moral in nature; they do not extend to what Professor MacKinnon describes as a political process, — discrimination against the female sex. The likelihood that the Supreme Court would permit the government to embark upon a venture to control speech in this area of politics, free from the restraints of the First Amendment, is most remote.

A second exception to the general rule that expression is entitled to the full protection of the First Amendment occurs in the case of expression by, or directed to, children. Thus in *New York v. Ferber* the Supreme Court upheld a New York statute which prohibited the use of children in "a sexual performance" and in aid of that provision prohibited dissemination of materials depicting sexual performances by children. The validity of such a measure rests upon the proposition that children are not and cannot be full participants in the system of freedom of expression. That system presupposes a maturity of understanding and judgment which children do not possess. As a result the Supreme Court has consistently applied different rules, in the area of expression and elsewhere, to children than those applicable to adults. It explicitly did so in the *Ferber* case, making it clear that the results would have been different were the statute not "limited to depictions of sexual activity involving children." Moreover, the Supreme Court has made it plain that the special rules pertaining to children cannot operate to infringe the First Amendment rights of adults.

Exceptions to First Amendment

Other exceptions to full protection under the First Amendment are based on doctrines pertaining to libel, clear and present danger, and regulation of the time, place and manner of expression. None of these theories justify the relaxation of the traditional guarantees of the First Amendment in the case of pornographic materials. Libel laws deal exclusively with the protection of reputation against false statements and are narrowly circumscribed. The clear and present danger exception is applicable only to advocacy which is "directed to inciting or producing imminent lawless action and is likely to incite or produce such action." Time, place and manner regulations are sanctioned primarily in situations where exercise of the right to freedom of expression creates a physical conflict with the exercise of other rights, such as the use of a public street for a demonstration in a way that interferes with normal traffic. In all these areas the First Amendment theories require that the exceptions be confined to narrow and concrete categories which have the least inhibiting effect upon the system of freedom of expression Creation of a vast new exception that would remove from the protection of the First Amendment all expression that tended to promote the subordination of women would, to the contrary, leave the system a shadow of its former self.

Political Analogy

The nearest analogy to what is proposed in the Minneapolis Ordinance would be an official enactment prohibiting all expression that promoted or encouraged racism in our society. The laws, constitutional and statutory, that attempt to eradicate racism in our national life have never been carried to such a point. They deal with discriminatory acts, not the expression of discriminatory beliefs, opinions, ideas or attitudes. And it is hard to believe that the Supreme Court would permit their extension into such areas. One is not likely to find the Supreme Court enjoining the performance of the *Merchant of Venice* or banning William B. Schockley from expounding his views on the inferiority of the Negro race. . . .

Censorship Imperils Freedom

As with Nazi rantings about Jews or racist trash spread by the Ku Klux Klan, speech graphically depicting the sexual humiliation and subordination of women is protected by the First Amendment because we have learned as a free people that it is impossible to censor speech we hate without imperiling the system of free expression upon which our political and social structure rests.

Harriet Pilpel, quoted in *Ms.*, April 1985.

Finally, it should be noted that the attempt to avoid First Amendment difficulties in the Minneapolis Ordinance by asserting, not that pornography causes discrimination, but that pornography "is" discrimination, cannot succeed. This device, which has been hailed as a new approach to the problem, is no more than a play on words. Pornography is speech or expression, as those terms are used in First Amendment theory, and like most expression has an impact upon attitudes and behavior. The question is whether, because of this impact, pornography can be proscribed. It does not help to eliminate the intermediate step in the legal analysis and declare that pornography "is" discrimination. . . .

The suppression of pornography through governmental intervention encourages the intolerance syndrome throughout a society. Civil liberties are, as is often said, indivisible. The legal doctrines, governmental machinery and attitudes which work for the suppression of speech in one area promote suppression in other areas. A program for censorship of pornography thus gives comfort to the forces of reaction and advances the cause of those who seek a closed society. The movement for gender equality has little to gain from such a climate of opinion.

Impractical Ban

One additional, overriding, consideration must be faced. The elimination of pornography by governmental censorship is simply not workable, at least by any democratic process. The area of prohibition is so vast, the machinery of civil litigation so cumbersome, the hope of changing attitudes by government decree so quixotic, that nothing positive is likely to be accomplished. Rather the results, in terms of selective enforcement, underground circulation of "violative materials," encouragement to organized crime, and the general discrediting of law enforcement, would be entirely negative. In the ensuing confusion the original problem will remain unsolved. . . .

An attempt to deal with the problem of pornography through governmental suppression would involve a dangerous emasculation of the First Amendment. The damage to our system of free expression would extend far beyond the area of pornography. Moreover, such an effort would almost certainly prove unworkable.

"Why take this remote and improbable route to arrive at a point—banning pornography—that one can reach directly by citing the venerable argument that pornography damages the moral fiber of society?"

Pornography Is a Moral, Not a Civil Rights, Issue

Charles Krauthammer

Charles Krauthammer, the author of the following viewpoint, is a senior editor for *The New Republic* and is widely published in other periodicals. In the following viewpoint he argues that banning pornography, which "damages the moral fiber of society," is a worthwhile goal. Antipornography civil rights laws, he says, are simply covering up the real nature of the pornography issue. By saying that rights will be expanded rather than reduced by such legislation, its proponents are camouflaging their real, and valid, goal of censorship.

As you read, consider the following questions:

1. What argument does Mr. Krauthammer say conservatives usually give in favor of banning pornography?
2. What argument does he say civil libertarians usually give against banning pornography?
3. Why does the author believe it would be better to openly advocate censorship of pornography than to misleadingly "disguise it as a campaign for civil rights"?

The intent of anti-pornography civil rights legislation is to do away with the blight of pornography. What can be wrong with that?

A good question, and an important one. Over the decades it has spawned a fierce debate between a certain kind of conservative (usually called cultural conservative) on the one hand and civil libertarians on the other. The argument went like this. The conservative gave the intuitive case against pornography based on an overriding concern for, it now sounds almost too quaint to say, public morality. Pornography is an affront to decency; it coarsens society. As Susan Sontag, not a conservative, writing in defense of pornography says, it serves to "drive a wedge between one's existence as a full human being and one's existence as a sexual being." The ordinary person, of course, does not need a philosopher, conservative or otherwise, to tell him why he wants to run pornography out of his neighborhood. It cheapens and demeans. Even though he may occasionally be tempted by it, that temptation is almost invariably accompanied by a feeling of shame and a desire to shield his children from the fleshy come-ons of the magazine rack.

That may be so, say the civil libertarians, but it is irrelevant. Government has no business regulating morality. The First Amendment guarantees freedom of expression, and though you may prefer not to express yourself by dancing naked on a runway in a bar, some people do, and you have no business stopping them. Nor do you have any business trying to stop those who like to sit by the runway and imbibe this form of expression. It may not be *Swan Lake,* but the First Amendment does not hinge on judgments of artistic merit or even redeeming value.

Clear Traditional Debate

Now this traditional debate over pornography is clear and comprehensible. It involves the clash of two important values: public morality *vs.* individual liberty. The conservative is prepared to admit that his restrictions curtail liberty, though a kind of liberty he does not think is particularly worth having. The civil libertarian admits that a price of liberty is that it stands to be misused, and that pornography may be one of those misuses; public morality may suffer, but freedom is more precious. Both sides agree, however, that one cannot have everything and may sometimes have to trade one political good for another.

Not the [anti-pornography civil rights] bill, and that is what made it so audacious—and perverse. It manages the amazing feat of restoring censorship, which after all is a form of coercion, while at the same time claiming not to restrict rights but expand them. The logic is a bit tortuous. It finds that pornography promotes bigotry and fosters acts of aggression against women, both of which, in turn, "harm women's opportunities for equality of rights in employment, education, property rights, . . . contribute significantly to restricting women from full exercise of citizenship . . . and undermine women's equal exercise of rights to speech and action."

Apart from the questionable logical leaps required at every step of the syllogism, the more immediate question is: Why take this remote and improbable route to arrive at a point—banning pornography—that one can reach directly by citing the venerable argument that pornography damages the moral fiber of society? Why go from St. Paul to Minneapolis by way of Peking?

Antipornography Legislation

Antipornography legislation is not censorship but regulation of community order and morality.

Editorial, *Christianity Today,* February 19,1982.

The answer is simple. As a rallying cry, public morality has no sex appeal; civil rights has. Use words like moral fiber and people think of Jerry Falwell. Use words like rights and they think of Thomas Jefferson. Use civil rights and they think of Martin Luther King Jr. Because civil rights is justly considered among the most sacred of political values, appropriating it for partisan advantage can be very useful. (The fiercest battle in the fight over affirmative action, for example, is over which side has rightful claim to the mantle of civil rights.) Convince people that censorship is really a right, and you can win them over. It won over the Minneapolis city council. And if to do so, you have to pretend that fewer rights are more, so be it.

Reversed Definitions

Civil rights will not be the first political value to have its meaning reversed. The use of the term freedom to describe unfreedom goes back at least as far as Rousseau, who wrote, without irony, of an ideal republic in which men would be "forced to be free." In our day, the word democracy is so beloved of tyrants that some have named their countries after it, as in the German Democratic Republic (a.k.a. East Germany). And from Beirut to San Salvador, every gang of political thugs makes sure to kneel at least five times a day in the direction of "peace." So why not abuse civil rights?

The virtue of calling a spade a spade is that when it is traded in, accountants can still make sense of the books. The virtue of calling political values by their real names is that when social policy is to be made, citizens can make sense of the choices. That used to be the case in the debate about pornography. If [anti-pornography civil rights legislation is] any indication of where that debate is heading, it will not be the case for long.

That is a pity, because while it is easy to quarrel with the method of the ban, it is hard to quarrel with the motive. After a decade's experience with permissiveness, many Americans have become acutely aware that there is a worm in the apple of sexual liberation. That a community with a reputation for liberalism should decide that things have gone too far is not really news. The call for a pause in the frantic assault on the limits of decency (beyond which lies the terra cognita of what used to be taboos) is the quite natural expression of a profound disappointment with the reality, as opposed to the promise, of unrestricted freedom. There are pushes and pulls in the life of the national superego, and now there is a pulling—back. Many are prepared to make expression a bit less free in order to make their community a bit more whole, or, as skeptics might say, wholesome.

Unashamed Censorship

That is nothing to be ashamed of. So why disguise it as a campaign for civil rights? (True, liberals may be somewhat embarrassed to be found in bed with bluenoses, but this case is easily explained away as a one-issue marriage of convenience.) In an age when the most private of human activities is everywhere called by its most common name, why be so coy about giving censorship its proper name too?

"There should be no shame in saying that pornography should be controlled."

Pornography Must Be Censored

Tottie Ellis and Peter McGrath

Tottie Ellis, the author of the first part of the following viewpoint, is vice president of the conservative organization, Eagle Forum. Peter McGrath, author of Part II, is a senior editor for *Newsweek* magazine. Both authors believe that in some way pornography must be controlled. In the following viewpoint, Ms. Ellis describes pornography as being an entirely negative force that menaces society. Mr. McGrath says that while it might have been acceptable to defend "harmless" pornography many years ago, it has become more and more bizarre, more and more brutal, and will continue to do so unless people refuse to accept it.

As you read, consider the following questions:

1. How does Ms. Ellis define pornography?
2. Why does Ms. Ellis see censorship, in this case, as being a positive action?
3. Why, according to Mr. McGrath, does pornography continue to become more deviant?
4. What solution, if any, does Mr. McGrath propose for the pornography problem?

America is swimming in a sea of filth and violence.

Under the banner of freedom, it has become fashionable to deify man, humanize God, demean women, and exalt sex and violence—in short, to reduce in our lives the dimensions of modesty, decency and privacy.

Twenty years ago, pornography was hard to find. Today it is difficult to avoid.

There is a flood of X-rated movies and nude centerfolds in magazines that exploit sex. Network television brags about cracking the last taboos, and cable TV channels show explicit R- and X-rated sex films.

The testimony in a rape trial that came into millions of homes recently had language so explicit that a national magazine raised the question: Is news becoming voyeurism?

Unhappy Freedom

Yet all this "freedom" has not made people happy. There is more sexual frustration in our society than ever before. There are fewer happy marriages, and more boredom and revulsion towards sex.

The efforts of the pornographers seem concentrated in two areas: undressing our bodies and unclothing our souls.

The so-called "openness trip" on which America has been embarked has created a tremendous outcry, especially from women, against the dehumanization that takes place when people are reduced to mere sexual objects.

Pornography is hard to define legally, but it does exist.

Pornography is anti-culture, anti-conscience, anti-God, anti-family, anti-child and anti-woman. Pornography brutalizes and insults society.

Surely something that is such a public menace can and should be regulated.

Regulating goes under many names. But if we don't like it, we call it censorship.

The Good of Censorship

Censorship is not the only answer, but it is part of the answer. Those who call for more control are not more righteous, but they do understand that society has the right to prevent or control that which brings about its own destruction.

We regulate narcotics, public safety, and the speed limit. Gambling and prostitution are banned in most places. But when controlling pornography is mentioned, supporters plead the First Amendment.

The First Amendment is never absolute. No one is granted total freedom. Common sense says there is a difference between free political expression and commercial entertainment aimed at shocking or embarrassing through vulgarity and violence.

It is difficult to work out the intricacies of each and every anti-pornography law. But as many cities are discovering—and as the new Indianapolis ordinance shows—it can be done and it must be done.

There should be no shame in saying that pornography should be controlled. Shame should be heeded—it is trying to tell us to act.

II

The late Kenneth Tynan, critic and author of "Oh! Calcutta!", the first play to bring open erotica to the legitimate stage, once wrote an essay called "In Praise of Hard Core." There he suggested that arousal of desire is one of art's functions, and that sexual stimulation is no less an artistic aim than arousal of desire for heroism, or virtue, or God. On what grounds, he asked, do we limit "art" to the abstract operations of the soul or the imagination? Why assume that "anything that appeals to the genitals belongs in the category of massage?" When a writer couples literary craft and sexual pleasure, Tynan wrote, "he is doing an artist's job." "The basic [artistic] criterion, in the case of pornography, is whether or not it succeeds in exciting us."

Quality of Democracy

If you care for the quality of life in our American democracy, then you have to be for censorship.

Irving Kristol, *Reflections of a Neoconservative*, 1983.

It was a courageous attempt at a head-on defense of pornography—no liberal ambivalence, no nose-holding orthodoxy (I personally hate this stuff but defend its right to exist). In the process, however, Tynan fell back on moral relativism: art is its own justification. But if art in pornography is a success in exciting us, what can be said about pornography in the 16½ years since Tynan's essay? He had in mind the "expertly titillating" novel "Fanny Hill," or perhaps something like the triple-X film "Misty Beethoven," a benign if crude parody of Shaw's "Pygmalion." In short: graphic sexual depiction but still good, clean fun. That was the hard-core pornography of its day. In the years since, the meaning of "hard core" has changed, at least in the United States. The boundaries have expanded. . . . In New York one popular porn "loop"—a short 35-mm film shown mostly in sex-arcade coin machines—is called "Scorcher of Hot Torture," and

194

is advertised as "super sadism at its cruelest . . . sublime agony."
. . . Even if such material succeeds in exciting people, would anyone call it art?

A "Normal Sexual Appetite"

Tynan presupposed a pornography consumer with a "normal"
sexual appetite. (He also presumed a man; most sexually explicit
material embodies male fantasies.) But for the possessor of a
healthy sexuality, the most likely response to such works—once
the first thrill fades—is boredom. This is particularly true of pornographic movies, which make the mechanistic, oil-rig aspects
of intercourse all too plain. The modern pornographer's fusion of
sex and violence, on the other hand, suggests a consumer with
an abnormal appetite—yet it was probably inevitable. "Our research shows that every time there is satiation of . . . themes,
people to some degree lose their ability to be aroused by it," says
psychologist Neil Malamuth of UCLA. "Therefore, newer
themes are introduced, breaking new taboos."

Behind the obvious point lies a subtle truth: if pornography did
not exist, we might have to invent it. As the great French sociologist Emile Durkheim pointed out 90 years ago, society *requires*
behavior that most people would call deviant. In other words,
"antisocial" conduct has a social function. Crime, for example,
is "an integral part of all healthy societies," according to Durkheim, because it unites law-abiding citizens in expressions of
outrage. By violating the collective values of the community, it
reminds the community of those values, and reinforces them.
"We have only to notice what happens, particularly in a small
town, when some moral scandal has just been committed,"
wrote Durkheim in his classic work "The Division of Labor in
Society." "[People] stop each other on the street, they visit each
other, they . . . wax indignant in common. From all the similar
impressions which are exchanged, for all the temper that gets itself expressed, there emerges a unique temper . . . which is
everybody's without being anybody's in particular. This is the
public temper."

Deviance Promotes Solidarity?

Durkheim's conclusion—however much it may affront common sense—is that deviance promotes solidarity. It establishes
the outer boundaries of permissible behavior and helps establish
a community's identity. But there is an important corollary to
this idea. As Yale University sociologist Kai T. Erikson put it in
"Wayward Puritans," an examination of the Salem witch hunts
from Durkehim's perspective, "Boundaries remain a meaningful point of reference only so long as they are repeatedly tested
by persons on the fringes of the group and repeatedly
defended." That is, "wrong" behavior must continue even as it

is being condemned and sometimes punished. Thus, no matter where a society draws its outer moral limits, deviant behavior will always arise on the other side. Expanding the boundaries calls even more extreme forms of deviance into existence, or at least into the public arena.

This seems to be what happened when American society extended the limits of acceptability for pornography. In a less permissive era, a movie like "Psycho" was inside the boundary (despite its famous shower scene). Russ Meyer's soft-core "Vixen" was on the line, and anything resembling "Misty Beethoven" was completely out of the question. There was no place in the social system for sadomasochistic films, for example. Whatever such material existed was kept well hidden. But the moment the likes of "Misty Beethoven" began to acquire legitimacy, kinkiness and violence crept into mass-market pornography—simply to establish that some things are still beyond the pale.

Refuse to Go Forward

Americans are ambivalent about pornography. They want access to conventional erotica while suppressing more extreme forms. But there is no going back: the law's acceptance of a hard core that now seems mild made room in the legal shadows for more brutal forms. We *can* refuse to go forward, however. Any outright embrace of those more brutal forms would create a new vacuum on the other side of the borderline—to be filled by material most of us cannot even imagine.

"Instead of calling for an end to porn, we should be seeking ways in which to make it better."

Pornography Should Not Be Censored

Barry W. Lynn and Al Goldstein

Barry W. Lynn, the author of Part I of the following viewpoint, is a legislative counsel for the American Civil Liberties Union. Al Goldstein, author of Part II, is the publisher and editor of *Screw*, a sexually explicit magazine. Both authors believe that, if there is a problem with pornography, censorship is not the way to deal with it. In the following viewpoint, Mr. Lynn discusses what he perceives as positive uses of pornography and questions whether the picture we are given of pornography as the brutalization and degradation of women is accurate. Mr. Goldstein comments on his belief that sexuality should be more fully explored than it is and states that it is repression, not expression, which is the threat to society.

As you read, consider the following questions:

1. According to Mr. Lynn, what is the most common subject of pornography?
2. What does Mr. Lynn claim are some of the positive uses of pornography?
3. Why does Mr. Goldstein believe that repression is more dangerous than pornography?

Barry W. Lynn, "Pornography's Many Forms—Not All Bad," *The Los Angeles Times*, May 23, 1985. Reprinted with the author's permission.

Al Goldstein, "Midsection Debate—Pornography: Love or Death?", *Film Comment*, December 1984. Reprinted with the author's permission.

I

The Justice Department has announced the creation of a new commission to study "the serious national problem of pornography." Although many Americans might agree with this assessment, this judgmental mandate starts the inquiry too far along the course.

Is More Worse?

There is unquestionably more pornography available today than 15 years ago. However, is it legitimate to assume that more is worse? Pornography is speech, words and pictures about sexuality. No one would consider an increase in the level of speech about religion or politics to be a completely negative development. What makes speech about sexuality different?

The examples used lately by anti-pornography advocates to characterize the phenomenon, such as "women hung on meathooks," do tend to skew the debate. We are led to believe that billions of dollars are spent each year primarily to purchase chronicles of bestiality and mutilation. Focusing on these conceals many other kinds of explicit material.

In truth, pornography comes in many forms, but its general themes are still consensual sex in a variety of places, couplings and positions. Pornography both reflects and encourages sexual fantasies, possibly the most intimate form of human expression. It offers messages that are understood by viewers in distinctive ways.

Female Subordination or "People Making It"?

Its critics accurately charge some of it with advocating the "subordination" of women, the very kind of repugnant message for which First Amendment protections are necessary. But does every centerfold really urge "subordination," or can it conceivably be an apolitical, aesthetic expression? A photo that theoretically fits the Women Against Pornography definition of acceptable erotica (depicting "mutual, respectful, affectionate, humorous and power-balanced" sexuality) may still just be a picture of "naked people making it" to a 17-year-old with a copy under his bedcovers.

Like it or not, the eye and mind of the sexual beholder remain highly individual.

Taken as a whole, pornography advocates sexual experimentation. It asserts the pleasure of human sexuality even if unaccompanied by affection, permanent reltionships, privacy, intent to procreate or responsibility. There is certain to be heated and lengthy debate about the morality and aesthetics of such conduct.

The First Amendment does not only protect speech that is socially useful; the American Civil Liberties Union takes no institutional stand on the "quality" of speech, pornographic or otherwise. However, the increased availability of sexually explicit speech might make some beneficial contribution to society, even if it resists elevation to the status of high art.

Positive Uses of Pornography

The failure to examine some of its uses could be dangerous. Pornography certainly plays a cathartic role at times. Does the masturbation that it assists for adolescents serve as a substitute for sexual activity that could be fare more detrimental, particularly for young women who risk pregnancy?

Similarly, Johns Hopkins therapist John Money notes, "Patients who request treatment in a sex-offender clinic commonly disclose that pornography helps them contain their abnormal sexuality within imagination, as a fantasy, instead of having to act it out in real life with an unconsenting, resentful partner, or by force." If it is legitimate to try to understand why pornography might trigger a rare individual to commit a crime of sexual violence, it is equally appropriate to try to understand how the material might prevent one.

Need to Discriminate

It makes no sense at all to me—that I am such a brainless fool that if I see a few violent movies I'll feel it's perfectly fine to go out and rape somebody. Are we that impressionable? That's the whole process of growing up. You're supposed to be able to discriminate.

Brian De Palma, interviewed in *Film Comment,* October 1984.

For others the material has a claimed sex-education function, teaching couples about the varieties of sexual response and stimulating mutual erotic interest. The increasingly graphic nature of the material is itself a repudiation of the idea that only certain body parts of one gender are attractive. Sexual expression is no longer limited to fascination with large breasts and aversion to male genitalia. This, too, may be seen as a healthy development, particularly since the 1970 commission found that pornography was so controversial because of the "inability or reluctance of people in our society to be open and direct in dealing with sexual matters."

Our society also breeds an unequal distribution of sexual experience. The myriad sexual opportunities open to those culturally defined as "beautiful" or "handsome" are denied to some who are shy, unattractive or physically disabled. The role of pornography in the lives of such lonely persons, for whom visual images must substitute for sexual experiences with partners, is also worth consideration.

A defensible inquiry by a new commission should take fully into account all the competing claims about the meanings, effects and significance of pornography, instead of proceeding doggedly on a moral crusade against fantasies.

II

As a maker of pornography, and as a champion of the rights of free expression, I've been called on again and again to defend sexually explicit material. Over the years, the censors, the bluenoses, the anti-sex forces have been presented in various guises: as Christians, as protectors of youth, and lately, more and more, as feminists. But these distinctions don't interest me very much. The difference between the fundamentalist and the feminist arguments against porn is verbiage; the underpinnings are the same. Sexual repressiveness is rooted in self-hate, self-loathing, in a Puritanical inability to enjoy the full sensuality of the body. . . .

With one exception, I take the First Amendment to be absolute, plenary. That exception concerns the sexualization of children; . . . I think Constitutional guarantees must be abrogated to that extent in order to protect our children. . . .

Porn and Violence Are Not Synonymous

The argument against violent porn has been very well refuted. . . .

There have been studies which show that representations of rape desensitize people to violence against women, but there have been no studies which show that non-violent pornography causes anything like a similar reaction. Time and again, studies either have shown that porn does *not* cause antisocial behavior or have failed to show that it does. Yet I am still seeing signs in anti-porn "Take Back the Night" parades: "Porn Is Violence Against Women." These people don't care about the truth; they care about their tenuously constructed, house-of-cards logic.

Let me reiterate: Pornography and violence against women are not conterminous, no matter how much feminist theorists say they are or wish they were. Edward Donnerstein, out of the University of Wisconsin, used sado-masochistic pornography in a study of its effects on men. And it turned out that it did desensitize his subjects to violence to some extent. Yet the Donnerstein study is trundled out repeatedly to indict *all* porn, including that with no S-M content. Donnerstein himself said if there are studies showing that non-violent porn causes desensitivity to abuse of women, he'd like to see them.

The feminist argument against porn feeds off just such hazy distinctions as the blurring of the line between S-M and non-violent porn. The rhetorical weight of the argument depends on that line being ignored. But it is on such distinctions that rational discourse and social decision-making ought to be based; otherwise we live in an Orwellian "Truth-is-lies" society. . . .

Why are the feminists so hysterical about pornography? One could see it as a single issue of the women's movement, maybe even a major issue, but *the* issue? I believe women who object so stridently to representations of explicit sexuality are reacting not on a political basis but on a moral basis. Women have been indoctrinated for centuries to hate sex, to fear it, above all to remain ignorant about it. That this is an element of male control over them may be true. But the result is that the feminists just cannot throw off the yoke of centuries in a generation, that when they see a picture of female genitals they just cannot stop themselves from saying "dirty"—afterward modified to "politically incorrect."

I was astonished that, in the controversy surrounding Vanessa Williams [1984's Miss America, deposed for modeling in a sex mag-

© Blaine/Rothco

azine photo feature,] it was always assumed she did something wrong by posing nude. She did nothing wrong. She celebrated her body by doing so. Yet the starting point in discussions about her is, "How could she do something so bad?" Puritanism is rampant in this society, and Puritanism has always been just as large an element in feminism as it has been in fundamentalism. . . .

It is the repression of sexuality which leads to rape, violence against women, and a host of other social ills. By agitating for censorship, for repressing that sexuality which porn represents (a flawed representation, to be sure), feminists and fundamentalists are prolonging an already too-long struggle for sexual freedom. Instead of calling for an end to porn, we should be seeking ways in which to make it better.

"Constitutional protection of free speech is content blind. Every person's voice is protected."

The First Amendment Forbids Censorship

Lois Sheinfeld

The so-called "Minneapolis ordinance" has become a national issue, debated by constitutional defenders, feminists, Moral Majoritarians, and others concerned about the effect of pornography on society. Lois Sheinfeld, an attorney and associate professor of journalism and mass communications at New York University, is a staunch defender of the constitutionally guaranteed right of freedom of expression. In the following viewpoint, she points out the dangers of enacting and enforcing a law such as the Minneapolis ordinance which, she believes, cannot be clearly, uniformly interpreted and which will threaten everyone's right to express unpopular or distasteful views.

As you read, consider the following questions:

1. Why does Ms. Sheinfeld believe the Minneapolis ordinance and similar laws are dangerous?
2. What does Ms. Sheinfeld think is vague about "subordination," the basic concept of the ordinance?
3. What does Ms. Sheinfeld think of the evidence often presented to prove that pornography causes violence against women?

Lois Sheinfeld, "Midsection Debate—Pornography: Love or Death?", *Film Comment*, December 1984. Reprinted with the author's permission.

"Suppression" Spinoza said, "is paring down the state till it is too small to harbor men of talent." These words, written over 300 years ago, precisely describe the anti-pornography censorship campaign now being waged against filmmaker Brian De Palma and others. While modern packaging cleverly disguises the new censors—the 1984 models come cloaked in civil rights theory—the mindset of those who would smother free thought and expression has not changed. Bookburners may wrap themselves in new rationalizations, but the books and films they condemn still burn.

The latest brand of censorship ordinances—passed in Minneapolis and vetoed by the mayor; enacted into law in Indianapolis—forbids pornography on the theory that it violates women's civil rights. Under the terms of this legislation, newspapers, literature, films, and visual art portraying the "graphic, sexually explicit subordination of women" are subject to governmental proscription. Not only motion pictures depicting violence against women, but all "pictures" or "words" in which women are presented as sexual objects for domination or conquest, as sexually submissive, or as degraded or inferior in a sexual context, can be suppressed.

Dangerous Departure From Free Speech

This anti-pornography legislation represents a radical and dangerous departure from accepted First Amendment principles. It permits any woman to demand the censorship of offending depictions without proving factually that they caused direct, immediate, serious harm—or, indeed, any harm at all—to her or to anyone else. According to the architects of the legislation, Catharine MacKinnon and Andrea Dworkin: "The systematic sexual subordination of the pornography *is* the injury." Thus, the purported justification for government censorship is not some demonstrated evil to which the publication of an idea will lead but rather the offensive nature of the idea itself, namely, "dehumanizing women as sexual things and commodities."

Further, the new laws plainly forbid portrayals of women that do not fall within the very limited category of expression which the courts have defined as obscenity. Literary and film classics found sufficiently demeaning to women under the sweeping, ill-defined provisions of the ordinances are now subject to repression.

But that is not the full measure of the danger. If the ordinances are sustained as constitutional, nothing in the theory that supposedly supports them would restrict censorship to "sexually explicit" material. Unlike laws against obscenity, where the arousal of prurient interest is the essential focus, here prohibition is based upon the "subordination" of a sex-defined class. A claim of "subordination" could as easily be leveled against a

204

treatise suggesting that a woman's place is in the home raising children, or against a film portrayal of a "dumb blond" (Marilyn Monroe in *Bus Stop* or *The Misfits*), or even a smart blond (Meryl Streep in *The Seduction of Joe Tynan*). And government "civil rights" censorship needn't be limited to the professed protection of women. Blacks, Poles, Jewish mothers, Orientals, "Moonies," *et al.* could equally claim that satirical, derogatory, or critical portrayals are suppressible as "dehumanizing" and "subordinating." First Amendment rights would be bounded by the sensibilities of every group in our pluralistic society.

ALL Voices Protected

Constitutional protection of free speech is content blind. Every person's voice is protected, not because we like or approve every "picture" or "word," but because we recognize that when official censors make the choice of what we see and hear, all speech is at risk. The authors of the Constitution understood that a democracy can flourish only when each of us decides the value and acceptability of ideas, not the government. Otherwise, demanded Thomas Jefferson: "Whose foot is to be the measure to which ours are all to be cut or stretched?"

Invoking governmental repression of disfavored expression is not unique to these times. We have a sorry history of attempts to override the fundamental First Amendment guarantees of free speech and press in order to impose an official guardianship over the public mind. As John Milton observed, censors have often tried to "starch" us into a gross conformity, and to change our open society into one in which the people hear only one voice and see only one image, that which the government in power seeks to put forward. Political dissenters and the proponents of unpopular views—advocates of civil rights, women's rights, and the nuclear freeze—have all suffered the assaults of censorship because some people thought their voices were "offensive," "repulsive," and "dangerous."

The First Amendment imperative of free expression protects our liberty against just such assaults. Justice Oliver Wendell Holmes made the essential point long ago: "The ultimate good desired is better reached by free trade in ideas—the best test of truth is the power of the thought to get itself accepted in the competition of the market. . . . That at any rate is the theory of our Constitution . . . we should be externally vigilant against attempts to check the expression of opinions that we loathe and believe to be fraught with death, unless they so imminently threaten immediate interference with the lawful and pressing purposes of the law that an immediate check is required to save the country."

Courts Are Vigilant Against Suppression

Courts have upheld this basic principle even when the speech at issue was, to most minds, hateful, dehumanizing, and subordinating. When television films broadcast the Ku Klux Klan disparaging blacks and Jews, the Supreme Court held in *Brandenburg v. Ohio* (1969) that the state could not punish this advocacy, absent a clear showing that the speech was directed at, and would likely produce, "imminent lawless action."

Similarly, when public officials attempted to forbid the neo-Nazi march through Skokie, Illinois, a suburb with a large Jewish population including several thousand survivors of the Nazi holocaust, the court upheld even the neo-Nazis' right of free speech. *Collin v. Smith* (1978). Despite the judges' "personal views" that the march would be "extremely mentally and emotionally disturbing" to many people, and "repugnant to the core values held generally by residents of this country," the court held: "However pernicious an opinion may seem, we depend for its correction not on the conscience of judges and juries but on the competition of other ideas"; this is what "distinguishes life in this country from life under the Third Reich." In the absence of evidentiary proof of intentional and direct incitement to violence, the Skokie march was constitutionally protected.

Insufficient Evidence

Some supporters of the anti-pornography ordinances claim that pornography causes rape and other acts of criminal sexual violence. This view ignores the state of the evidence. There have been two comprehensive studies of the supposed link between pornography and sex crimes: the investigations of the President's Commission on Obscenity and Pornography (1970), and the British Committee on Obscenity and Film Censorship (1979). Both concluded that there was no causal nexus between pornography and crime. That finding is further buttressed by studies of actual sex offenders.

As for the recent rash of laboratory research done under artificial conditions (conducted by academic psychologists on student subjects who received extra credit in their psychology courses), suffice it to say here that Professors Edward Donnerstein and Neil Malamuth, whose studies are most often cited by would-be pornography censors, admit that the research data does not establish a direct causal connection between pornography and sexual violence. They do not advocate censorship legislation.

Failure of Proof

Anti-pornography censors are simply unable to meet the evidentiary burden imposed by the First Amendment upon those who seek to suppress expression on the ground that it causes serious harm. They should not be permitted to sidestep this profound failure of proof by the legerdemain of declaring that pornography is *per se* a violation of women's civil rights.

Filmmaker Brian De Palma said, "I'd hate to live in a world where art is left in the hands of the political people. I'd leave the country if it came to that—sounds like Russia." Indeed it does. In August of this year, the Moscow Communist Party Committee criticized the Soviet film studios for straying from Socialist Realism and issued new directives requiring filmmakers to reflect current problems and workers' lives. A month later, Soviet Party leader Konstantis U. Chernenko had this to say: "Freedom of creative work cannot be a privilege for a few. Nothing and no one can free a person from the compulsory demands of society, its laws that are obligatory for all. It is naive to think that one can blacken the moral and political foundations of our system. . . . The nation will not forgive anyone defection to the side of our ideological opponents. . . ."

Such government control over the content of expression is an anathema in a democracy. What De Palma sees and paints onto his "white canvas" might not be to everyone's taste. But the state may no more proscribe his creative work than it may prescribe his artistic images.

In Luis Bunuel's succinct phrase: "A pox on censors!"

"No lawyer who has ever studied the First
Amendment would ever claim that we have an
absolute right to freedom of speech."

The First Amendment
Does Not
Protect Pornography

Janella Miller

Janella Miller, an attorney with the Legislative Action Committee
of the Pornography Resource Center in Minneapolis, believes that
pornography is an unquestionable threat to society's safety. In the
following viewpoint she states that a law such as the Minneapolis
ordinance would make producers and sellers of pornography more
accountable to the community. Ms. Miller is convinced that courts
would tend to interpret the law narrowly rather than broadly,
thereby not threatening other forms of free expression.

As you read, consider the following questions:

1. Why does the author believe that pornography is not merely
   pictures, words, and ideas but "a *practice* that harms women
   and children"?
2. Antipornography laws are often criticized for being too vague
   or open to too many interpretations. How does Ms. Miller
   think the Minneapolis ordinance is an answer to this
   problem?
3. Ms. Miller seems to claim that the Minneapolis ordinance and
   similar laws are not forms of censorship. How does she
   justify this claim?

Janella Miller, "Midsection Debate—Pornography: Love or Death?", *Film Comment*,
December 1984. Reprinted with the author's permission.

The latest movie in the stream of Hollywood offerings in which women are brutally murdered has arrived—*Body Double*. Director Brian De Palma's attitude toward the violence and toward the encroachment of pornography into the mainstream media demands a response. De Palma told interviewer Pally that he opposes pornography legislation because he has a right as an individual to take pictures of anything he pleases, including pictures of a woman being violently murdered with a drill. He says that he does not believe viewing pornography has any effect upon male viewers or their likelihood of committing acts of aggression against women.

De Palma has obviously not been paying any attention to the victims of pornography, the *women* who are hurt by and through pornography, who have courageously spoken out about the abuse they have experienced because of pornography. Nor has he studied the most recent research linking pornography to increased aggression against women. If he had, he would know that pornography is not just ideas or words or pictures on a page; it is a *practice* that harms women and children.

Pornography as Discrimination

Recent legislation passed in Minneapolis and in Indianapolis addresses, for the first time, the harm done by pornography. Feminist writer and activist Andrea Dworkin and University of Minnesota law professor Catharine MacKinnon, at the request of the Minneapolis city council, wrote a civil rights ordinance on pornography that defines pornography as a form of sex discrimination and as a violation of women's civil rights. The ordinance defines pornography as "the sexually explicit subordination of women, graphically depicted, whether in pictures or in words," that also includes one or more of nine listed characteristics which range from "women are presented as sexual objects who enjoy pain or humiliation" to "women are presented in postures of sexual submission or sexual servility, including by inviting penetration" to "women are presented being penetrated by objects or animals."

Material must meet *each* part of the definition to be pornography. It must be graphic, *and* sexually explicit, *and* subordinate women, *and* meet at least one of the nine characteristics. If the material is found to meet the definition of pornography, the ordinance provides for a civil cause of action if a woman is coerced into making pornography, has pornography forced upon her in her workplace or any other context, or is assaulted or attacked in a way that is caused by a specific piece of pornography. The ordinance also provides for a claim against the makers, exhibitors, distributors, and sellers of pornography for the terrorism and intimidation created by pornography which perpetuates women's inferior status and promotes continued discrimination against women in all areas of our society. A woman could bring her claim directly to court or to the city civil rights commission, which would decide whether to pursue the matter further. Because the ordinance creates a civil cause of action, a judge could award damages or issue an injunction against the further sale of the pornography, but he or she could not order a criminal penalty. The ordinance does not give more power to the police. It *does* give more power to women.

Harm to Women

By acknowledging the harm done to women and providing them with a way to do something about that harm, the ordinance goes beyond any previous legislation. The ordinance is not an obscenity law and does not contain any of the language of obscenity laws which rely upon criminal sanctions to enforce community standards of decency. The theory behind this ordinance is diametrically opposite to the theory behind obscenity laws.

Insult to Constitution

Pornography is not a "victimless crime" and it is an insult to our Constitution to allow the profiteers of pro-rape propaganda to wrap themselves in the First Amendment.

Phyllis Schlafly, *Union Leader*, October 12, 1984.

The ordinance says that women have a right to possess their bodies and their lives. Obscenity laws, on the other hand, are based upon the premise that women's bodies are dirty, that sex is immoral, and that pornographic materials should be kept behind closed doors where only men over the age of 18 can have access to them. Under obscenity laws, a judge must decide whether the "average person, applying contemporary community standards" would find that the work, taken as a whole, appeals to prurient interest. That usually means that a work is "obscene" when a man is sexually aroused. Because of their vagueness, obscenity laws have been haphazardly and erratically applied. Nowadays, we seldom hear cries of censorship about obscenity, which is not protected speech under the First Amendment, perhaps because the laws do not work.

Accountability, Not Censorship

There have been many, however, who claim that the civil rights ordinance on pornography is censorship. They misunderstand what the ordinance does and also what censorship means in a society that values freedom of speech. The word *censorship* implies official examination of pictures, plays, television, etc., for the purpose of suppressing parts deemed objectionable on moral, political, military, or other grounds. The ordinance works on an entirely different principle. There are no prior restraints, no criminal penalties, and no increase in police powers. A particular work could be removed only after an adversarial hearing before a judge. Both sides could present evidence, as in any legal case. The ordinance provides no mechanism for telling people that they *cannot* publish what they want. What it *does* do is tell pornographers that if they print material in which women and children are harmed, or material that *leads* to harm or discrimination, they must be responsible for the harm that they cause. In that regard, the ordinance works much like libel laws which hold the media accountable for false information that harms an individual if the individual can prove that he or she was injured.

If the ordinance were effectively applied, pornographers would undoubtedly choose not to publish certain materials because it would be too costly for them. There *would* be fewer pornographic pictures, movies, and books. Supporters of the ordinance intend that result. For the first time, people are challenging the idea that the First Amendment should shield pornography from any legal challenge. The harm done to women in this legal system is great enough to justify limitations on the pornographers' right to "freedom of speech" under which they have committed atrocities against women for centuries.

Right to Freedom Not Absolute

Those who cry censorship whenever someone mentions the ordinance act as though the right to freedom of speech were absolute and that it exists in a vacuum apart from any other social concern. But no lawyer who has ever studied the First Amendment would ever claim that we have an absolute right to freedom of speech.

We have libel laws, slander laws, and court decisions which limit words that create a "clear and present danger" or that constitute "fighting words." Obscenity is not protected speech under the First Amendment, nor is child pornography. In *New York v. Ferber*, 458 U.S. 747 (1982), the Supreme Court said that the *harm done* to children in pornography justified restricting the pornographers' right to print what they please. There is thus a precedent for weighing the harm done to *women* against the pornographers' right to "freedom of speech." That harm was well documented in the hearings before the Minneapolis city council in December 1983 and the Senate Sub-committee on Juvenile Justice in September 1984.

Social scientists, researchers on pornography, people who work in the field of sexual assault, and victims of pornography

211

have all testified about the effects of pornography. Using this documentation to support legislation and legal decisions would not be a new idea. The Supreme Court has used sociological data in the past, most notably in *Brown v. Board of Education*, to support their finding that the harm done to black children in segregated schools was so great that integration was required to alleviate it.

Worst Outcome Not Likely

Opponents of the ordinance are also fond of claiming that we are on a slippery slope that will end in the suppression of the Bible or of Shakespeare. The concern about the Bible and Shakespeare is very interesting, since they are not sexually explicit and would not be covered under the ordinance as it is written. But opponents also seem to be arguing that *any* limitation on freedom of speech will lead to the institution of a repressive regime.

Marketing Empty Values

No one wants to be accused of being a prude, right? But what kind of society are we permitting to grow up around us? Can an "innocent" $3 thrown away for one copy of *Penthouse* help seduce another 18-year-old young woman into a life of emptiness, a future with no values? . . . Does U.S. freedom mean the right to market anything, anywhere, anytime?

Nicholas J. Penning, *National Catholic Reporter*, December 31, 1982.

These arguments are based not upon facts about the ordinance or upon a reasoned analysis of the First Amendment, but rather upon the manipulation of people's fears. Forecasting the worst possible outcome for any piece of legislation is an old legal strategy that is particularly powerful when the predicted outcome is the suppression of ideas. However, it does not necessarily follow that the worst possible outcome will occur *because* we are in the area of the First Amendment. In fact, the opposite outcome is more likely. Americans guard their right to freedom of speech with a tenacity that would surprise people in other countries which also value their freedom of speech. A judge would likely interpret the ordinance narrowly, finding that material falls under the ordinance only if it clearly degrades and subordinates women.

We always trust the courts to make decisions which clarify and illuminate the law. To say that the task is difficult begs the question. Asking the courts to decide which works subordinate women and which works fall within the definition of pornography, when a woman claims to be harmed, will be far less onerous than asking them to decide which works are "obscene" under obscenity laws or what constitutes "discrimination" under civil rights laws. There is actually much less potential for abuse under the ordinance than there is under obscenity laws, under which we allow judges to make moral decisions about what we should view. Under the ordinance, as written, morality plays no role. The ordinance speaks only to the subordination of women and the harm done to women in pornography. I fear more the continuation and legitimation of a system which treats women as less than human, as objects to be consumed, than I do allowing our judges to decide what is covered under a specific and narrow definition of pornography.

An amendment to the ordinance further prevents frivolous abuses of the trafficking provision by precluding legal actions based upon isolated passages or isolated parts. The ordinance does not specify a certain percentage of the work that must be pornographic to be actionable, but the authors clearly intend to require more than a *de minimum* amount.

Finally, the ordinance avoids any interpretation leading to the suppression of *ideas* by defining pornography as "the sexually explicit subordination of women, graphically depicted, whether in pictures or in words." Pornography does not present the "idea" of subordination or of any other idea. It is an active *practice* of subordination. Only pictures and words that *do* subordinate women are pornography and fall within the scope of the ordinance.

Solution Cannot Wait

We cannot wait for a solution any longer. Pornography has grown into an $8 billion-a-year industry that has spread into every form of media and advertising. America's culture has become pornographic. It is time to look at the harm done by pornography and weigh it against the pornographers' claimed right to freedom of speech. We legislate for the good of society—to establish justice, equality, and freedom for all Americans. But women still do not have justice, equality, or freedom. The pornographers tell lies about women which lead to terrorism and intimidation. Men rape and torture women with the use of pornography. Men force women to perform in pornography. A beaten and tortured woman is not free, nor is she an equal member of our society. She is a second-class citizen with no way to improve the daily condition of her life, because no one hears her screams.

Distinguishing Bias from Reason

The subject of pornography often generates great emotional responses in people. When dealing with such a highly controversial subject, many will allow their feelings to dominate their powers of reason. Thus, one of the most important basic thinking skills is the ability to distinguish between statements based upon emotion and those based upon a rational consideration of the facts.

Most of the following statements are taken from the viewpoints in this chapter. Consider each statement carefully. *Mark R for any statement you believe is based on reason or a rational consideration of the facts. Mark B for any statement you believe is based on bias, prejudice, or emotion. Mark I for any statement you think is impossible to judge.*

If you are doing this activity as a member of a class or group, compare your answers with those of other class or group members. Be able to explain your answers. You may discover that others will come to different conclusions than you. Listening to the reasons others present for their answers may give you valuable insights in distinguishing between bias and reason.

If you are reading this book alone, ask others if they agree with your answers. You will find this interaction very valuable.

> R = *a statement based upon reason*
> B = *a statement based on bias*
> I = *a statement impossible to judge*

1. Pornography is a systematic practice of exploitation that harms women.
2. Child pornography is banned because children are not mature enough to exercise reasoned judgment about participation in sexual activities.
3. The suppression of pornography through government intervention (censorship laws) encourages the intolerance syndrome throughout a society.
4. The elimination of pornography by governmental censorship is simply not workable.
5. Pornography is an affront to decency; it coarsens society.
6. Because civil rights is justly considered among the most sacred of political values, appropriating the term to fight pornography can be very useful.
7. Civil rights will not be the first political value to have its meaning reversed; the use of the term "freedom" to describe unfreedom goes back at least as far as Rousseau.
8. The virtue of calling political values by their real names is that when society policy is to be made, citizens can make sense of the choices.
9. America is swimming in a sea of filth and violence.
10. Twenty years ago, pornography was hard to find; today it is difficult to avoid.
11. Pornography is hard to define legally, but it does exist.
12. No matter where a society draws its outer moral limits, deviant behavior will always arise on the other side.
13. If it is legitimate to try to understand why pornography might trigger a rare individual to commit a crime of sexual violence, it is equally appropriate to try to understand how the material might prevent one.
14. Sexual repressiveness is rooted in self-hate, self-loathing, in a Puritanical inability to enjoy the full sensuality of the body.
15. Pornography and violence against women are not the same thing no matter how much feminists say they are.
16. By agitating for censorship, feminists and fundamentalists are prolonging an already too-long struggle for sexual freedom.
17. Every person's voice is protected by the Constitution because we recognize that when official censors make the choice of what we see and hear, all speech is at risk.

Periodical Bibliography

The following list of periodical articles deals with the subject matter of this chapter.

Melinda Beck and others	"A Court Test for Porn," *Time*, August 13, 1984.
Mary Kay Blakely	"Is One Woman's Sexuality Another Woman's Pornography?" *Ms.*, April 1985.
Alan Dershowitz	"One Cure for an X-Rated Problem," *The Washington Times*, June 7, 1985.
Edward Donnerstein and Daniel Linz	"Sexual Violence in the Media: A A Warning," *Psychology Today*, January 1984.
Lisa Duggan, Nan Hunter, and Carol S. Vance	"False Promises: New Antipornography Legislation in the U.S.," *SIECUS Report*, May 1985. Available from the Sex Information and Education Council of the U.S., 80 Fifth Avenue, Suite 801-2, New York, NY 10011.
Jean Bethke Elshtain	"The New Porn Wars," *The New Republic*, June 25, 1984.
Film Comment	Special section debating "Pornography: Love or Death?" December 1984.
Freedom to Read Foundation	"Foundation Challenges Indianapolis Anti-Pornography Ordinance," *Freedom to Read Foundation News*, Volume 12, Number 4. Available from 50 East Huron Street, Chicago, IL 60611.
Robert Halfhill	"Pornography, Free Speech and Gay Separatism," *Gay Community News* (Boston), December 8, 1984.
Harper's	"Forum: The Place of Pornography," November 1984.
Nan D. Hunter	"Anti-Pornography Measure Could Backfire on Women," *Los Angeles Times*, March 21, 1985.
Mary Jonigan	"Confronting Pornography," *Maclean's*, October 29, 1984.
Del Martin	"An Open Letter to Feminists About Anti-Pornography Laws," *Gay Community News* (Boston), May 4, 1985.
Vidy Metsker	"The Curse of Pornography," *Psychology for Living*, March 1985.

Jon Garth Murray	"For Mature Audiences Only," *The American Atheist*, March 1984.
National Decency Reporter	"Obscenity is a 'Victimless Crime?' " May/June 1982, and "Memorandum on Methods to Halt Distribution of Obscene Television Video Cassettes," March/April 1983. Available from Citizens for Decency Through Law, Inc., 2331 West Royal Palm Road, #105, Phoenix, AZ 85021.
Aryeh Neier	"Expurgating the First Amendment," *The Nation*, June 21, 1980.
Mary Pellauer	"Personal Perspective," *Christianity and Crisis*, May 13, 1985.
Aric Press	"The War Against Pornography," *Newsweek*, March 18, 1985.
Elayne Rapping	"Banning Pornography Solves No Problems and Worsens Some," *Guardian*, December 19, 1984.
Lois P. Sheinfeld	"Banning Porn: The New Censorship," *The Nation*, September 8, 1984.
Curtis V. Stomer	"Curbing Media Sex and Violence by Means Other than Censorship," *Christian Science Monitor*, May 25, 1985.
USA Today	"Fighting Smut, Pros and Cons," May 1, 1985.
Robert Wright	Letter, *Harper's*, February 1985.

Organizations to Contact

American Civil Liberties Union
132 W. Forty Third St.
New York, NY 10036
(212) 944-9800

The ACLU champions the rights set forth in the Declaration of Independence and the Constitution. They oppose banning pornography and any other form of expression. The ACLU publishes a quarterly newsletter, *Civil Liberties*; a legislative newsletter, *Civil Liberties Alert*; a booklet, *Why the ACLU Defends Free Speech for Racists and Totalitarians*; as well as several handbooks, public policy reports, project reports, civil liberties books, pamphlets on the Freedom of Information Act, and reports on the abortion issue.

American Library Association
50 E. Huron St.
Chicago, IL 60611
(312) 944-6780

The ALA supports intellectual freedom and free access to libraries and library materials. The ALA's affiliated offices are the Office for Intellectual Freedom, which publishes *Newsletter on Intellectual Freedom*, and Freedom to Read Foundation, which works for the legal and financial defense of intellectual freedom. The ALA publishes a Banned Books Week Kit, *Censorship Litigation and the Schools*, *Intellectual Freedom Manual*, pamphlets, articles, audiovisual products, and the annotated bibliography, "Pressure Groups and Censorship."

American Right to Read
c/o PEN American Center
47 Fifth Avenue
New York, NY 10003
(212) 255-4009

Founded in 1982, The ARR is a collection of authors working to fight censorship in America's public schools. The ARR offers teachers, parents, school administrators, and concerned community members the opportunity to "call upon authors who are eager to defend their own and other books in the communities that challenge them." They publish an irregular newsletter.

Association of American Publishers
One Park Avenue
New York, NY 10016
(212) 689-8920

The Association is a collection of producers of hardbound and softbound general, educational, trade, reference, religious, scientific, technical, and medical textbooks; instructional materials; systems of instructions; classroom periodicals; maps, globes, tests, and software. The AAP sponsors Publishing Forum, an informal discussion group, and compiles statistics. This organization bestows the Curtis G. Benjamin Award for creative publishing. It publishes a monthly newsletter.

Citizens Communication Center of the Institute for Public Representation
c/o Georgetown University Law Center
600 New Jersey Avenue NW
Washington, DC 20001
(202) 624-8047

CCIPR represents citizens and community groups attempting to remind the broadcast industry that it is a trustee for the public. The Center seeks to open the regulatory process to procedures and participation by citizens. It also aids citizens and groups without resources or technical skills in participating in the regulatory and decision-making processes and obtaining media access. In addition, it informs citizens and community groups of their right to participate in the decision-making process and to have access to the broadcast media. The Center educates and trains advocates to assert these rights.

Citizens for Decency through Law
2331 Royal Palm Rd., Suite 105
Phoenix, AZ 85021
(602) 995-2600

CDL seeks to assist law enforcement agencies and legislatures in enacting and enforcing Constitutional statutes, ordinances, and regulations controlling "obscenity and pornography, and materials harmful to juveniles." They work to create an awareness in the American public of the "extent and harms associated with the distribution of pornography through newsstands, bookstores, theatres, and television." CDL provides free legal assistance in the form of legal research, briefs, model legislation and courtroom assistance for obscenity prosecutions and civil action. They also conduct seminars for police and prosecutors on search and seizure, trial tactics, evidence and proof, and appeals. They enter appellate cases with friend-of-the-court beliefs "in support of law enforcement" and publish the bimonthly *National Decency Report*.

Clean Up TV Campaign
5807 Charlotte Avenue
Nashville, TN 37209
(615) 356-4367

The Campaign is composed of religious and civic groups, churches, and other interested parties. Their purpose is to insist that television programs be revised "so that they are no longer an insult to decency and a negative influence on young people." They have initiated a campaign to boycott products on programs "which depict scenes of adultery, sexual perversion or incest or which treat immorality in a joking or otherwise favorable light." The Campaign emphasizes that "this is clearly not censorship, but simply responsible action since companies remain free to sponsor any programs they choose." It publishes a monthly newsletter.

Committee for National Security
2000 P St. NW, Suite 515
Washington, DC 20036
(202) 833-3140

The Committee, founded in 1980, promotes change in the direction of national security policy through debate on alternatives to military confrontation and appropriate foreign policy. It publishes position papers, briefs, and reports.

Constitutional Rights Foundation
1510 Cotner Avenue
Los Angeles, CA 90025
(213) 473-5091

The CRF works "for improved and more meaningful teaching of the Constitution, especially the Bill of Rights and the legal and criminal justice system in public and private schools. The Foundation assists in in-service training for teachers, the development of student and/or teacher internships in government and the justice system, organizing student peer-teaching programs, and designing student and teacher conferences and workshops. They established Law, Education, and Participation (LEAP) to provide consulting services to public, professional, and educational agencies in organizing and implementing classroom and community programs on law, the legal process, and citizenship education for young people." It publishes the *Bill of Rights Newsletter*, *Education for Participation Manual*, *Bill of Rights Sourcebook*, student pamphlets, and role-playing simulation games.

Council on Interracial Books for Children
1841 Broadway, Rm. 500
New York, NY 10023
(212) 757-5339

The Council promotes children's books and other learning materials which are free of bias based on race, sex, age, or physical handicap. They review new children's books, television programs, and films and conduct studies. The Council develops criteria enabling teachers to identify and counteract racism and sexism in classroom materials. They also administer the Racism and Sexism Resource Center for Educators which develops and disseminates anti-racist, anti-sexist teaching materials, books, pamphlets, lesson plans fact sheets, and audio-visual materials. The Council publishes a monthly magazine, *Bulletin*.

Eagle Forum
Box 618
Alton, IL 62002
(618) 462-5415

The Forum is a spiritually motivated group supporting the "Holy Scriptures as providing the best code of moral conduct yet devised." They fight against forces that are anti-family, anti-religious, anti-morality, anti-children, anti-life, and anti-self-defense. They oppose ratification of the Equal Rights Amendment because they claim it is inconsistent with the rights of women, families, and individuals. Their plans include increasing tax exemptions for children, ending what they call unfair tax discrimination against the traditional family which now exists in the Individual Retirement Accounts, and rebuilding a strong national defense. They publish the monthly *Phyllis Schlafly Report* and the periodic Eagle Forum *Newsletter*.

Educational Freedom Foundation
20 Parkland, Glendale
St. Louis, MO 63122
(314) 336-1585

The Foundation disseminates information concerning education freedom via publications, conferences, and radio and television programs. EFR supports litigation defending freedom of choice in education without total loss of tax benefits. The Foundation conducts research and compiles statistics. The foundation publishes the semiannual *Educational Freedom* and also booklets.

First Amendment Congress
c/o Jean H. Otto
Rocky Mountain News
400 W. Colfax
Denver, CO 80204
(303) 892-5478

The First Amendment Congress is a group of journalism and communications-related associations with a total of 50,000 members; universities and newspapers. Their objectives are to enhance the awareness of all Americans that the First Amendment to the US Constitution guarantees them the rights of free speech and a free press, to convey the belief that a free press is not the special perogative of print and broadcast journalists but a basic right that assures a responsive government, to establish a dialogue between the press and people across the country, to encourage better education in schools about the rights and responsibilities of citizenship, and to obtain broader support from the public against all attempts by government to restrict the citizen's right to information. It attempts by government to restrict the citizen's right to information. It conducts local, state, and national First Amendment Congresses that involve the public in efforts to find solutions to problems of media credibility and public perceptions about the media's accuracy, fairness, objectivity, and thoroughness. It publishes a newsletter, brochures, and booklets.

Feminist Anti-Censorship Taskforce
Box 135
660 Amsterdam Ave.
New York, NY 10025

FACT is a feminist/activist group opposing proposed anti-pornography laws based on civil rights arguments. They also oppose all forms of censorship relating specifically to women. FACT believes that the anti-pornography laws "are a misguided, dangerous, and ineffective strategy in the battle against sexism and violence." The taskforce supports equal rights legislation, affirmative action, and non-sexist education.

Freedom to Read Foundation
50 E. Huron St.
Chicago, IL 60611
(312) 944-6780

The Foundation is a collection of individuals, associations, corporations, and other organizations concerned with protecting and defending freedom of speech and freedom of press. They seek to promote the recognition and acceptance of libraries and protect the public right of access to them, to support the right of librarians to make available to the public any creative work legally acquired, and to supply legal counsel and other support to librarians and libraries suffering legal injustices by reason of their defense of freedom of speech and freedom of press. It publishes the quarterly *News*.

Fund for Free Expression
36 W. 44th St.
New York, NY 10036
(212) 840-9460

This organization is a collection of journalists, writers, editors, publishers, and concerned citizens dedicated to preserving intellectual freedom throughout the world. It serves as the US sponsor for the British publication *Index on Censorship*, which reports on violations of free expression. The Fund sponsors educational and public policy projects to protect rights proclaimed in Article 19 of the Universal Declaration of Human Rights, conducts forums, and maintains the Americas Watch Committee which monitors and promotes observance of human rights in the Western Hemisphere. It publishes *Americas Watch Report*.

Morality in Media, Inc.
475 Riverside Dr.
New York, NY 10115
(212) 870-3222

MIM opposes traffic in pornography and indecency in media and encourages more vigorous enforcement of obscenity laws. They do not believe in censorship or prior restraint by the government. It publishes *Morality in Media Newsletter, Hill-Link Report of the Presidential Commission on Obscenity and Pornography*, legal publications, and pamphlets, including *You Can Help Stop the Pornography Traffic* and *Cliche Arguments and Answers*.

Moral Majority
305 6th St.
Lynchburg, VA 24504
(804) 528-5000

The Moral Majority is a political movement founded in 1979 by Rev. Jerry Falwell dedicated to convincing morally conservative Americans that it is their duty to register and vote for candidates who agree with their moral principles. Rev. Falwell organized the Moral Majority to respond to developments such as the legalization of abortion, the spread of pornography, and agitation for homosexual rights-developments which the movement feels indicates that the US is experiencing a "terrible moral decline." They do not specifically endorse candidates by name, but strive through letters, leaflets, and mass rallies to make clear where candidates stand relative to issues important to the group. This organization publishes the monthly newspaper, the *Report*.

National Coalition Against Censorship
132 W Forty-third St.
New York, NY 10036
(212) 944-9899

NCAC is an alliance of organizations committed to defending freedom of thought, inquiry, and expression by engaging in public education and advocacy on national and local levels. Their publications include a newsletter, *Censorship News*, and *Report on Book Censorship Litigation in Public Schools*.

National Coalition on Television Violence
P.O. Box 2157
Champaign, IL 61820
(217) 359-8235

The Coalition is an educational and research organization committed to decreasing the amount of television and film violence. It publishes *Film Review Weekly, News,* analyses of amount of violence in specific television programs and movies, and research and educational materials.

National Federation for Decency
P.O. Drawer 2440
Tupelo, MS 38803
(601) 822-8462

This organization promotes "the biblical ethic of decency in American society with a primary emphasis on television." It urges viewers to write letters to networks and sponsors protesting shows seen to promote "violence, immorality, profanity and vulgarity" and encouraging the airing of programs which are "clean, constructive, wholesome and family oriented." They compile statistics on television sex, profanity, and alcohol use. The Federation publishes a monthly newsletter.

National Obscenity Law Center
475 Riverside Dr.
New York, NY 10115
(212) 870-3232

The Center is a national clearinghouse of information on obscenity law for prosecutors, governmental agencies, and attorneys. They maintain a Brief bank, a compilation of all opinions on obscenity cases since 1808, and publish *Obscenity Law Bulletin.*

P.A.R.E.N.T.S.
c/o Jil Wilson
6706 Third Ave.
Kenosha, WI 53140
(414) 654-6867

People of America Responding to Educational Needs of Today's Society is a group of individuals organized to support academic excellence in schools, parents' rights, local control of schools, and the operation of private and public schools without federal controls. They oppose secular humanism and its programs in the schools and seek to awaken parent interest in and responsibility for education. They monitor state and federal legislation that affects public and private education, parents' rights and the family. They also encourage parents to inform legislators of their desire to control what children are taught. The Society publishes a newsletter and alerts when necessary.

People for the American Way
1424 16th St. NW, Suite 601
Washington, DC 20036
(202) 462-4777

PAW is a project of Citizens for Constitutional Concerns. It is a collection of religious, business, media, and labor figures committed to reaffirming the traditional American values of pluralism, diversity, and freedom of expression and religion. PAW does not engage in political or lobbying activity. PAW developed out of concern that an anti-democratic and devisive climate was being created by groups that sought to use religion and religious symbols for political purposes. They seek to help Americans maintain their belief in self, to reaffirm that in this society the individual still matters and that to improve the quality of life we must strengthen the values that unite us as humans and as citizens. PAW is engaged in a mass media campaign to create a positive climate of tolerance and respect for diverse people, religions, and values. It distributes educational materials, leaflets, and brochures.

Project Censored
Sonoma State University
Rohnert Park, CA 94928
(707) 664-2149

The Project is an annual media research project which explores and publicizes important new stories that have been overlooked or under-reported by the national news media. Each year the Project publishes the pamphlet *The Ten Best Censored Stories of the Year.*

Scholars and Citizens for Freedom of Information
c/o John Anthony Scott
School of Law
Rutgers University
Newark, NJ 07102
(201) 648-5687

SACFI is a group of political and social scientists, economists, sociologists, anthropologists, historians, jurists, and others in the academic community. They support the Freedom of Information Act in maintaining and protecting the nation's records and in guaranteeing public access to them, and promote a greater understanding of the Freedom of Information Act as a key research tool and as a protective instrument for the vital interests of a democratic society. It publishes a bimonthly newsletter and an irregular bulletin.

225

Women Against Pornography
358 W. 47th St.
New York, NY 10036
(212) 307-5055

WAP is a feminist organization founded by author Susan Brownmiller which seeks to change public opinion about pornography so that Americans no longer view it as socially acceptable or sexually liberating. They offer tours of New York's Times Square district, which they consider "the porn capital of the country," to women and men of all ages and backgrounds. The tour is intended to show firsthand that "the essence of Pornography is about the degradation, objectification, and brutalization of women." They also offer adult and high school slide shows/lectures which show how pornographic imagery pervades popular culture. WAP publishes a quarterly newsletter.

Women Against Violence Against Women
543 N. Fairfax Avenue
Los Angeles, CA 90036
(213) 648-8350

WAVAW is an activist, feminist collective working to stop the use of images of physical, sexual, and mental violence against women in mass media in order to end the "real world" violence it promotes. They sponsor public education, consciousness-raising and mass consumer action. Their current focus is pressing for policies of social responsibility that exclude using sexist/violent images of women in advertising and the media. They seek to educate people about sexist and violent exploitation in media and advertising. WAVAW publishes a quarterly newsletter.

Young Americans for Freedom
Box 1002
Sterling, VA 22170
(703) 450-5162

This organization is a bipartisan, political youth organization which seeks to promote the conservative philosophy of free enterprise and strong national defense. It publishes the quarterly *Dialogue on Freedom, New Guard,* and *YAF in the News* as well as reports.

Bibliography of Books

American Civil Liberties Union — *Free Speech, 1984.* Available from the American Civil Liberties Union, 132 West 43rd Street, New York, NY 10036.

American Civil Liberties Union — *Free Trade in Ideas.* Available from the Center for National Security Studies, 122 Maryland Avenue, NE, Washington, DC 20002 or the ACLU.

American Civil Liberties Union — *Why the American Civil Liberties Union Defends Free Speech for Racists and Totalitarians.* Pamphlet available from the American Civil Liberties Union.

Association of American Publishers, Inc. — *Limiting What Students Shall Read.* Available from 2005 Massachusetts Avenue NW, Washington, DC 20036.

Campaign for Political Rights — *The Freedom of Information Act. Why It's Important and How to Use It.* Available from Campaign for Political Rights, 201 Massachusetts Avenue NE, Washington, DC 20002.

Francis Canavan — *Freedom of Expression: Purpose as Limit.* Durham, NC: Carolina Academic Press, 1984.

Council on Interracial Books for Children — *Guidelines for Selecting Bias-Free Textbooks and Storybooks.* New York: Council on Interracial Books for Children, 1984.

John H. Court — *Pornography: A Christian Critique.* Downers Grove, IL: Intervarsity Press, 1980.

Donna A. Demac — *Keeping America Uninformed: Government Secrecy in the 1980's.* New York: Pilgrim Press, 1984.

Donald Alexander Downs — *Nazis in Skokie.* Notre Dame, IN: Notre Dame Press, 1985.

Fred W. Friendly — *The Good Guys, the Bad Guys, and the First Amendment.* New York: Random House, 1977.

Fred W. Friendly and Martha J.H. Elliott — *The Constitution—That Delicate Balance.* New York: Random House, 1984.

Neil Gallagher — *The Porno Plague.* Minneapolis: Bethany House, 1982.

Morton H. Halperin and Daniel N. Hoffman — *Top Secret.* Washington, DC: New Republic Press, 1977.

James C. Hefley	*Are Textbooks Harming Your Children?* Milford, MI: Mott Media, 1981. Available from Mott Media, Box 236, Milford, MI 48042.
Nat Hentoff	*The First Freedom: The Tumultuous History of Free Speech in America.* New York: A Laurel Book/Dell Publishing Co. 1980, 1981.
Douglas A. Hughes, ed.	*Perspectives on Pornography.* New York: St. Martin's Press, 1970.
Michael Jacobson, Robert Atkins and George Hacker	*The Booze Merchants: The Inebriating of America.* Washington: Center for Science in the Public Interest, 1983.
Laura Lederer, ed.	*Take Back the Night: Women on Pornography.* New York: Bantam, 1980.
Leonard W. Levy	*Emergence of a Free Press.* New York: Oxford University Press, 1985.
Herbert McClosky and Alida Brill	*Dimensions of Tolerance: What Americans Believe About Civil Liberties*, New York: Basic Books, 1984.
Richard B. McKenzie	*Bound to Be Free*, Stanford, CA: Hoover Institution Press, 1982.
Connaught Coyne Marshner	*Blackboard Tyranny.* New Rochelle, NY: Arlington House, 1978.
David Martin	*Screening Federal Employees.* Washington, DC: The Heritage Foundation, 1983.
Linda Melvern, David Hebditch, and Nick Anning	*Techno-Bandits: How the Soviets Are Stealing America's High-Tech Future.* Boston: Houghton-Mifflin Company, 1984.
Aryeh Neier	*Defending My Enemy: American Nazis, the Skokie Case and the Risks of Freedom.* New York: E. P. Dulton, 1979.
Office for Intellectual Freedom of the American Library Association	*Intellectual Freedom Manual.* Chicago: American Library Association, 1983.
Barbara Parker and Stefanie Weiss	*Protecting the Freedom to Learn.* Washington: People for the American Way, 1983.
Ithiel de Sola Pool	*Technologies of Freedom.* Cambridge, MA: The Belknap Press of Harvard University Press, 1983.
Stansfield Turner	*Secrecy and Democracy: The CIA in Transition.* New York: Houghton-Mifflin, 1985.

Index

230

232

234